Spammers, Scammers and Social Engineers

by Charles Conway

Keeping you safe online...

www.scam-detectives.co.uk

Copyright Information:

Limitation of liability/disclaimer of warranty:

ISBN 978-1-4716-3580-9

About the Author:

Charles Conway is a professional web designer based in Wrexham, North Wales.

As well as running his web design business, he is the editor of scam awareness website Scam Detectives (www.scam-detectives.co.uk) which was created in January 2010 to educate Internet users about the dangers of online scams and security threats.

As of January 2011 the website had received over 250,000 visitors from around the World and in July 2010 was short-listed for a Nominet Internet Award in the "Making the Internet Safer" category alongside such projects as the Vodafone Parents Guide, Cybermentors, E-Crime Wales and the Business Crime Reduction Partnership.

Charles is regularly asked to comment on news stories about online security and scams, and visits schools and community groups to talk about Internet safety for children and adults alike.

Contents

Introduction:

Early scam artists

The concept of dishonesty is certainly not a new phenomenon. Since time began, man has traded with man. In prehistoric caves and mud dwellings around the world, those skilled at hunting would trade meat and hides with those able to create tools and weapons in return for their wares.

As societies evolved, so did the concept of currency, moving from the trading of stored commodities to monetary transactions involving coins forged from bronze, silver and gold and the accumulation of wealth became a powerful motivation for the traders.

Even in these early civilisations, there were those who would take advantage of their fellow man to gain something for nothing or give less than promised to their customers. These early conmen would pad out sacks of potatoes with rocks to increase their weight, use subtle sleight of hand to cut short lengths of cloth or even create their own coins made of worthless metals that looked like the genuine article.

Early English literature makes references to dishonest people selling worthless goods for a hefty profit. Geoffrey Chaucer (1343-1400), author of The Canterbury Tales, tells of a "Pardoner", a medieval priest who would offer absolution to sinners in return for cash. The Pardoner boasts to his fellow travellers of having sold sacred objects which were in fact pigs bones as opposed to the bones of departed saints as he claimed.

The first "Con Man"

Despite these early mentions, the label of "Con Man" was not used until the trial of American criminal William Thompson in 1843.

Mr Thompson had an unusually direct method of ripping off his victims, involving engaging strangers in conversation until he had established sufficient rapport to ask them if they had enough confidence in him to lend him their watch.

When the hapless "mark" handed over his treasured timepiece, William would simply put it in his pocket and leave.

This may seem like a ludicrously simple approach to scamming, yet many people are taken in every year by similar ruses even now.

Examples include the "good samaritan scam", where a well dressed businessman approaches a stranger on the street claiming to have been mugged and asking if he can borrow a few pounds for the train fare home, promising to return the money as soon as he can get a replacement bank card. Of course, the money is never returned, and the conman will repeat the scam many times over the course of a day, netting hundreds of pounds for a few hours "work".

Mr Thompson's direct approach is not one that is favoured by the majority of ripoff merchants. The most lucrative cons are those whereby the victim does not realise that he has been duped at all, or only realises once it's too late to do anything about it. Because many scams pull the victim into a scenario which may be legally questionable, they often go unreported.

The Internet Age of Scamming

As technology and services have evolved in modern times, the methods used by conmen have also become more sophisticated.

Now that reliance on the Internet for commercial transactions and communication has become widespread, it has been embraced by scammers as a cheap and efficient way of reaching hundreds of thousands of potential victims in the time it takes to craft an email.

The availability of word processing, graphic design and web design software has enabled fraudsters to create convincing and credible documents, websites and credentials to help them deceive their victims even more effectively than ever before.

Throughout this book, you will see examples of fake websites and authentic looking emails purporting to come from banks and official organisations that have been used to great effect by real scammers.

By the time you've finished reading, you may feel that you simply can't take anything you see online at face value and that you never want to touch your computer again.

This is not my aim.

In writing this book I hope to give you more confidence to use the fantastic resource that is the Internet to further your business whilst encouraging you to exercise extreme caution when you are inevitably faced with the temptation of getting involved in that "once in a lifetime" opportunity to make some extra money for a minimal effort.

Looking closer to home

Before we explore the methods used by confidence tricksters, hackers and social engineers to convince you to part with your money, you need to be aware of some of the IT related threats to your business operation that could come from within your own organisation. In the first chapter, we'll look at some of those threats and how you can start to protect your business from insiders who may damage or compromise your data security, either maliciously, dishonestly or completely by accident.

The threat from within

Your staff probably have access to a computer, which is connected to a central server. Your server will contain all of the data that your staff need to do their job, but it probably also contains highly sensitive information that should be restricted to the partners or directors of your Company. If that data is compromised either by accident or design, unauthorised users could get their hands on information that could be used to damage your business.

In this chapter we'll explore how a member of staff could cause significant problems by gaining inappropriate access to your Company data.

The UK's *Computer Misuse Act (1990)* introduced three specific criminal offences which are of particular concern to businesses. They are:

---

1. Unauthorised access to computer material

2. Unauthorised access with intent to commit or facilitate commission of further offences

3. Unauthorised modification of computer material

Enough of the legal jargon, what does that actually mean?

OK, let's take them one at a time.

1. Unauthorised access to computer material

This is pretty self-explanatory. If there's information held on a computer system that someone is not supposed to have access to and he looks at it when he knows he shouldn't, he's committed a criminal offence.

To be convicted of an offence it must be proven that the offender knew that he shouldn't be looking at the information he accessed **at the time that he tried to access it.**

Example 1

Steve has just started a new job. He has been given access to the computer system but the firm's IT consultant has incorrectly assigned higher security privileges to Steve's account. As a result Steve accidentally gains access to confidential information which should be restricted to the partners of the firm.

Was an offence committed here?

Steve did not deliberately try and gain access to this information and could not have known that he was not authorised to view it. As such **no offence was committed.**

Example 2

John suspects that his bosses are thinking about firing him. The office is open plan so he knows they haven't been talking about him openly but thinks they may have exchanged emails discussing his performance. John surreptitiously watches his manager enter his email username and password then logs into his manager's account later that day to read his emails.

Was an offence committed here?

John was fully aware that he did not have permission to view his manager's emails when he used the stolen account details to log in. **In this case it is very clear that an offence was committed.**

Unauthorised access to computer material is not restricted to emails or data in the workplace. Anyone who **knowingly** obtains access to an email account, social networking profile, file server, laptop, personal digital assistant, mobile phone, voicemail or any other computerised data held in any form without consent is guilty of an offence.

It's also not limited to hackers or those with a traditionally criminal intent. Have you ever taken a peek at your partner's private messages when they've forgotten to log out of Facebook? **Guilty.** Checked out their text messages without permission? **Guilty.** Logged into their mobile phone voicemail account to listen to their messages? **Guilty.**

How can you protect your business from this type of offence?

Remember that this offence only applies to those who gain unauthorised access to information but **don't do anything else with it.** As such, it's probably both the least serious of the offences (and the easiest to protect against as the perpetrator is probably a) less technologically able than the average hacker and b) has some level of physical access to your systems.

The key to protecting your data from this type of attack lies in three major areas:

1) **Ensuring appropriate levels of access to Company data** by implementing levels of security clearance. It goes without saying that the office junior should have less access to Company data than the MD, but this often isn't the case.

2) **Enforcing a strong password policy.** See **page 63** for more details on creating more secure passwords and keeping them safe.

3) **A 'log off' policy** which should dictate that anyone leaving their computer terminal for any reason (regardless of how long for) should 'log off' to protect their machine from unauthorised access.

By making sure that your staff only have access to the data and applications they need to carry out their duties, keep strong passwords secure and log off from their terminals when they're not in use you can protect your Company from those who want to sneak about and find out how much their co-workers are REALLY earning, what the Sales Director says about the MD behind his back and why the legal secretary doesn't work there anymore….

2. Unauthorised access with intent to commit or facilitate commission of further offences

This is both a more serious offence under the Act (punishable by up to 10 years in prison) and is potentially more damaging to your business.

This section describes a scenario whereby someone both intentionally accesses unauthorised information **and** intends to use it to commit a further criminal offense such as fraud, harassment or theft. Offenders under this section of the Act can be prosecuted for both the actual crime committed, and the offence of unauthorised access with intent at the same time.

Example 1

Dave is the Company accountant and uses his work PC to check the Company's bank balance online. Dave struggles to remember the username and password for the bank website so keeps them written down in his desk diary. Whilst Dave is on lunch, James copies these details from Dave's diary and later logs in to the Company bank account, transferring £500 to his own account.

As well as committing the offence of theft, James has also committed an offence under this section of the Act because he used his unauthorised access to the Company online banking account to commit the theft.

Example 2

Craig has been fired from his position at a sales Company. Although he has returned his laptop and mobile telephone, he later realises that his remote access privileges have not been revoked and he logs into the Company server and downloads a complete list of the Company's clients which he then sells to a competitor.

Because Craig is no longer employed by the Company it is obvious that any subsequent access to Company systems or data is unauthorised. As such, Craig has committed both theft of the Company data and an offence under this section of the Act.

How can you protect your business from this type of offence?

This type of criminal activity can be very damaging to your business and a determined offender will try and bypass controls that you put in place to protect yourself. As such is it imperative that you implement strong security measures to prevent unauthorised access to financial information and sensitive Company data. As well as the damage to your business that could occur if sensitive information is stolen, the Data Protection Act puts a responsibility on business owners to use all reasonable measures to protect sensitive data and the Information Commissioner has the power to impose almost unlimited fines for failure to take adequate precautions against data loss under any circumstances.

1) **Make use of security devices offered by your bank**. Some banks offer a security 'key' to enable access to your online accounts. This device generates a random security code which must be entered along with your username and password to gain access to the account. The code expires after (usually) one minute and without it nobody can access your account.

2) **Ensure that your IT acceptable use policy** forbids your employees from keeping written records of usernames and passwords. They should be encouraged to generate strong passwords that they will be able to remember. See **page 63** for more details on creating strong passwords and keeping them secure.

3) **Operate good IT housekeeping.** When a member of staff leaves (or is fired) you should ensure that any remote access they had as part of their employment is revoked immediately so they cannot access your Company systems. You should also ensure that any passwords that may have been known to the employee (such as that of colleagues they may have covered for in the event of sickness or absence) are also changed. If the employee worked in the IT department or had administrative access to your server you should also ensure that your system is checked for any "back door" access which may have been installed surreptitiously.

4) **Install a strong firewall.** This will prevent hackers from gaining access to your Company systems and stealing sensitive data.

5) **Train your staff on spotting "phishing" scams.** A 'phishing' scam will attempt to trick you into revealing your access codes for online banking websites. See **page 21** for more information about this type of attack.

6) **Control the use of removable storage devices.** As well as the risk of accidental data loss, removable storage devices such as USB memory sticks, CD ROM disks and even MP3 players can facilitate the theft of data from your company. See **page 61** for more details about controlling the use of removable media devices in your business.

By ensuring that strong security protocols are in place, including sensible password policies, and that full records are kept of who has access to your Company systems from outside the premises, you can go some way to protecting your business from unauthorised access and data theft.

This will not however stop a determined criminal from stealing from your Company from the inside and you should ensure that your recruitment procedures include diligent checking of references and satisfactory explanations (including evidence) for any significant breaks in employment history. Did your potential new employee **really** spend a year travelling in Europe or was his sabbatical at Her Majesty's Pleasure?

3. Unauthorised modification of computer material

This section of the act is wide ranging and deals with any scenario where Company data is deleted, moved, destroyed, altered or otherwise made inaccessible. It can include the creation or distribution of computer viruses, accessing personnel records to change someone's pay grade, delete records of disciplinary action or alter staff appraisals, or the unauthorised addition of passwords to documents or folders to prevent somebody accessing them.

Example 1

Sally is a financial adviser within a High Street bank. It has been alleged that during a telephone conversation with a client she advised him to invest in shares in a particular Company which subsequently crashed, causing him to lose a significant amount of money. The client alleges that Sally did not adequately advise him of the risk in investing in the shares and is holding her responsible. The bank operates a call recording system and all telephone calls are held on a central server which all employees have access to for training purposes. Sally logs into the call recording system and deletes the recording of the call with this particular client, thereby destroying any evidence of her negligence.

Was an offence committed here?

Although Sally's access to the call recording system was authorised, it is clear that her action in deleting the call was not. As such, she has committed an offence under this section of the Act.

Example 2

Lisa's role within the Company has been made redundant and she is working her notice period. During her employment, Lisa created a bespoke database system which the sales team relies upon in the day to day performance of their duties. At 4.55pm on her last day, Lisa modifies the database so that it requires a password to access the data contained within it and does not advise anybody of this password, in the full knowledge that the sales team will be unable to function without it.

Was an offence committed here?

Whilst Lisa added the password to the database whilst still employed by the Company, her failure to provide the password to anybody within the Company (therefore denying them access to the data) constitutes an unauthorised modification of computer data and subsequently an offence under this section of the Act.

How can you protect your business from this type of offence?

As with all security arrangements, prevention is better than cure and there are several steps you can take to protect your business from this type of activity.

1) **Take nightly backups of all critical data.** This will ensure that in the event of a virus infecting your systems, or a deliberate attack by a hacker or disgruntled employee causing any loss or alteration of your data, the loss will be minimised and data can be restored once the situation has been remedied. Backups should be encrypted and store securely away from Company premises.

2) **Ensure appropriate access permissions are applied.** If employees are to have access to sensitive data such as recordings of telephone calls then ensure that their access is "read only". Where interactions with clients are recorded in a 'notes' section of your client database, you should also ensure that these are 'read only' once the note is committed to the system. This will prevent employees from modifying them later to support their own version of events should there be a dispute about 'who said what to whom'

3) **Install and maintain strong anti-virus software**. Viruses can cause catastrophic data loss and can be notoriously hard to remove. Using a strong anti-virus solution on your network (and ensuring it is set to update automatically every day) will protect your system from most attacks. Removable media such as USB flash drives or CD ROMS should also be scanned for viruses before every use.

4) **Hold "exit meetings" when a member of staff leaves.** Ensure that you hold a meeting with any member of staff is leaving (or is fired) to make sure that they have given up any critical passwords before they receive their final salary. Check that these passwords are current by logging into any password protected files or accounts that they have access to and revoke their IT security clearance on their last day to make sure they don't cause any issues before they go.

This type of offence can again be very damaging to your business, as unauthorised destruction or modification of data could expose your Company to intervention from regulatory bodies, impede your ability to defend a claim of negligence against you or, in extreme circumstances, prevent your business from operating at all.

By ensuring that your employees are contractually bound by effective IT policies and your systems are protected by appropriate anti-virus solutions, file access permissions and nightly backups, you can protect your business from a potentially catastrophic loss of data.

In this chapter we've concentrated on some of the ways that your employees could commit electronic crimes in your workplace, acting with either mischievous, curious, devious or even overtly criminal intent to invade colleague's privacy, access information to which they have no legitimate right of access or even to steal money or Company assets electronically.

Thankfully, computer crimes emanating from within your organisation are relatively rare. A much greater threat to your IT security comes from accidental exposure to viruses or malicious software (malware) and from social engineering techniques which seek to trick you into revealing personal information which should be kept private.

We'll look at those threats in the next chapter.

Spyware, Phishing and Viruses

Social Media

"Social Media" is a term that describes any website that allows you to connect with friends or colleagues and share news, gossip, photos and videos with your contacts. Examples of social media websites include Facebook, Myspace, LinkedIn and Twitter.

From a business perspective, these websites can be a great way to engage your customers and promote your latest products and services, as well as a tool for reputation management. An unhappy customer posting a comment about your Company on a social media website can present an opportunity to show just how customer focussed you are by responding in a positive, constructive manner to help the customer resolve their issue.

Social media can also be a huge drain on productivity. A recent survey by employment website MyJobGroup.co.uk showed that 6% of Great Britain's 34 million workers spend at least an hour a day on these websites.

Not only does this cost your business money, it also places your IT infrastructure at risk of accidental infection by viruses, spyware and malicious software which could in turn result in data loss, information theft or physical damage to your systems.

How does Social Media put your business at risk?

Your employee sees a status update from one of their friends, a link on Twitter, or an advert on their Facebook profile that promises a funny video, sexy pictures or salacious gossip about a popular celebrity.

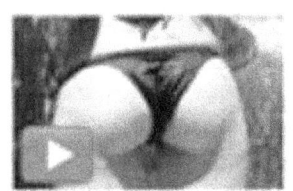

Distracting Beach Babes [HQ]
Length: 5:32

2 hours ago via MPEG · Comment · Like · See Wall-to-Wall

Eager for some further distraction from work, he clicks on the link and is taken to a page that says something like this:

MEDIA PLAYER NOT DETECTED

In order to view this video you must update your media player

click here to install the update

Cursing the IT department for not keeping the computers up to date, he clicks on the link to download the update. Rather than downloading the media player update and delivering the afore-promised sexy beach babes video , the site downloads a piece of malicious software to his computer.

Types of malicious software

Fake Anti-Virus

This type of malware will try and convince you that there is a virus on your computer that must be removed. It carries out a 'scan' of your system and reports several threats that can only be removed by purchasing an expensive removal tool.

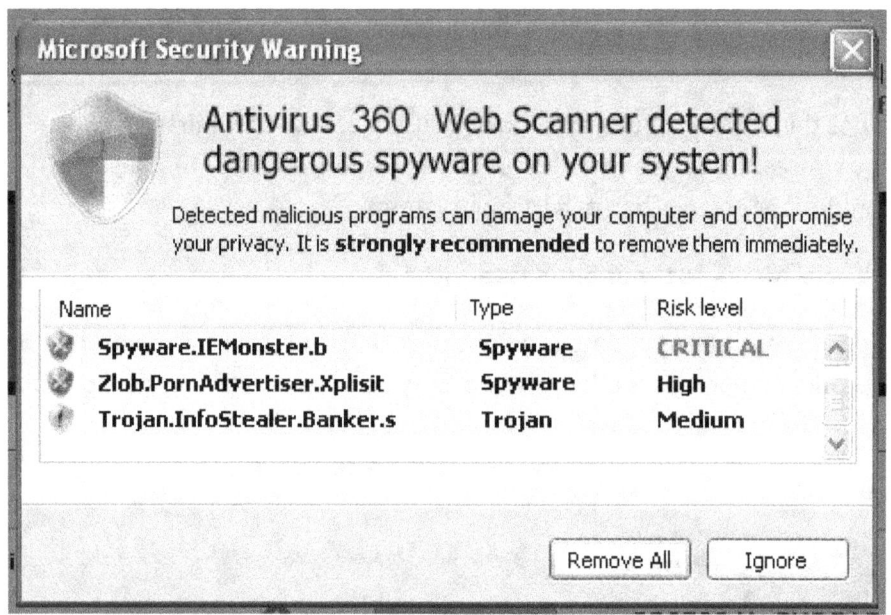

In reality, there is no virus on your system (apart from the ones that the malware has installed itself) and if you pay for the tool to remove them you'll just lose your money. This type of malware can be highly disruptive as if you ignore it, it will continue to display popups warning of more and more virus infections. It can be very difficult to remove and you'll probably need to bring in a specialist to clean your system.

Spyware

Spyware comes in many forms and it's effects can vary in terms of severity. At best it will record the websites visited on an infected computer, building up a profile of the user's interests to deliver targeted advertising via pop-up screens which are distracting and can cause your computer to run slower than usual.

At worst it could take the form of a keylogger, which records every keystroke made on the computer, giving a hacker access to every username and password used on the system.

This could leave you vulnerable to theft of confidential data or banking details or even give the hacker access to the inner workings of your Company website, enabling them to take it down or access your customer's personal details, including their credit card data.

Computer Viruses

Again, viruses can take many forms and vary in the severity of their impact on your computer, but the worst kinds can have disastrous effects, including the complete eradication of all data on your hard drive. Worse still, before activating themselves, some viruses will access your email address book and send themselves to all of your contacts, including your customers, suppliers and colleagues.

We'll look at some more ways that viruses can get onto your computer later.

Zombies

We're not talking about "Night of the Living Dead" here. In IT circles, a Zombie is a computer that has been infected with a particular type of virus that will allow a hacker to use it to do several things:

1) **Send out spam email.** A Zombie computer will be used to send hundreds of thousands of emails advertising everything from fake watches to drugs promising to enhance sexual performance. Not only will this result in your computer running more slowly because of all the emails being sent in the background, but it could damage your reputation as your Company email address will be associated with spam activity. It could also result in your Internet Service Provider withdrawing service and cutting off your Internet access or even in criminal investigation.

2) **Orchestrate attacks against websites.** Distributed Denial of Service (DDOS) attacks are often carried out using networks of Zombie computers. Late in 2010, hackers orchestrated DDOS attacks against financial institutions such as Mastercard and Paypal to stop their websites working after they withdrew payment facilities from the whistleblowing website Wikileaks. This worked by using massive Zombie networks to bombard the website with millions of fake visits, to overload the servers and stop legitimate users being able to access the site. Again this could result in you losing access to the Internet or being investigated by the Police.

3) **Host illegal websites.** Many websites hosting illegal content such as images of child abuse, "phishing" sites (see **page 21** for more details about "phishing") and even entire online shops selling fake or non-existent goods have been found to be hosted on Zombie networks.

Rogue Diallers

Less common with the advent of "always on" Internet access, this type of malware will use your computer's modem to connect to premium rate services over the Internet, costing you up to £1.50 a minute. Many websites will tell you that Broadband users are unaffected by this type of software, but if you leave your computer's dialup modem connected so you can use your PC to send faxes, or as a backup in case your Broadband connection fails, you could still be affected.

URL Injectors

Difficult to find and even more difficult to remove, a URL Injector will monitor your web browser looking for requests for specific websites, such as online banking sites, social networks and online auctions. When you type in, for example "www.mybank.com" the malware will detect this request and intercept it, sending you instead to a fake website that looks just like your bank website but is actually designed to steal your login details, allowing the hacker to access your bank account at his leisure.

How can you protect your business from viruses and malware?

Up to date Internet security software can help to protect your systems from becoming infected, and you should ensure that your anti-virus solution is set to update at least once a day. Unfortunately no anti-virus package is 100% foolproof. Online security firm Panda reports that 37,000 new variants of virus and malware are detected by their analysts every single day.

The key to protecting your business and its IT infrastructure from virus infection is the introduction of strong acceptable use policies and the education of your staff in the ways that they can avoid accidentally exposing your systems to these kinds of threat.

- Ensure that your staff are fully aware of the implications of downloading unauthorised software or updates to their computers.

- Introduce an acceptable Internet use policy and ensure that all staff are aware of what they can and cannot do on your computers.

- If you decide to restrict access to social media websites you should do this at server level to ensure that unauthorised access is not possible from any computer on your network.

- Encourage your staff to monitor the performance of their computer and report any unexpected activity or slowing down of the machine.

- Watch out for "Bouncing Email". Reports of "undelivered emails" that you have not sent are often a sign that your computer has been sending out spam messages without your knowledge.

- Set your anti-virus software to update every day and to scan your computers for viruses at least once a week.

- Make sure that your computer's operating system is up to date and all security patches are installed automatically.

- Install and maintain a strong firewall to protect your system from outside access.

Email threats

"Phishing"

Most of the organisations you come into contact with during your everyday business activities will be encouraging you to carry out your business with them online. Online banking is almost universal now and increasingly Her Majesty's Revenue and Customs and Companies House are encouraging business owners to file their statutory returns over the Internet. This is good news, as it reduces the amount of time spent filling in paper forms, waiting in queues and writing cheques.

That's fine as long as businesses can trust that the websites they are visiting in order to carry out these transactions are genuine and will keep their details secure.

"Phishing" attacks will try and convince you to visit a website which is an almost exact replica of your bank's site, or the HMRC gateway, with the express intention of tricking you into revealing your login credentials or other personal details so they can steal your money.

How does it work?

Online Banking

You receive an email from your bank informing you of a new message, suspicious transaction or security update that requires you to log in to your account. It looks genuine, containing your bank's logo and details of their registered office and telephone number. It may even contain a security warning telling you to look out for suspicious emails.

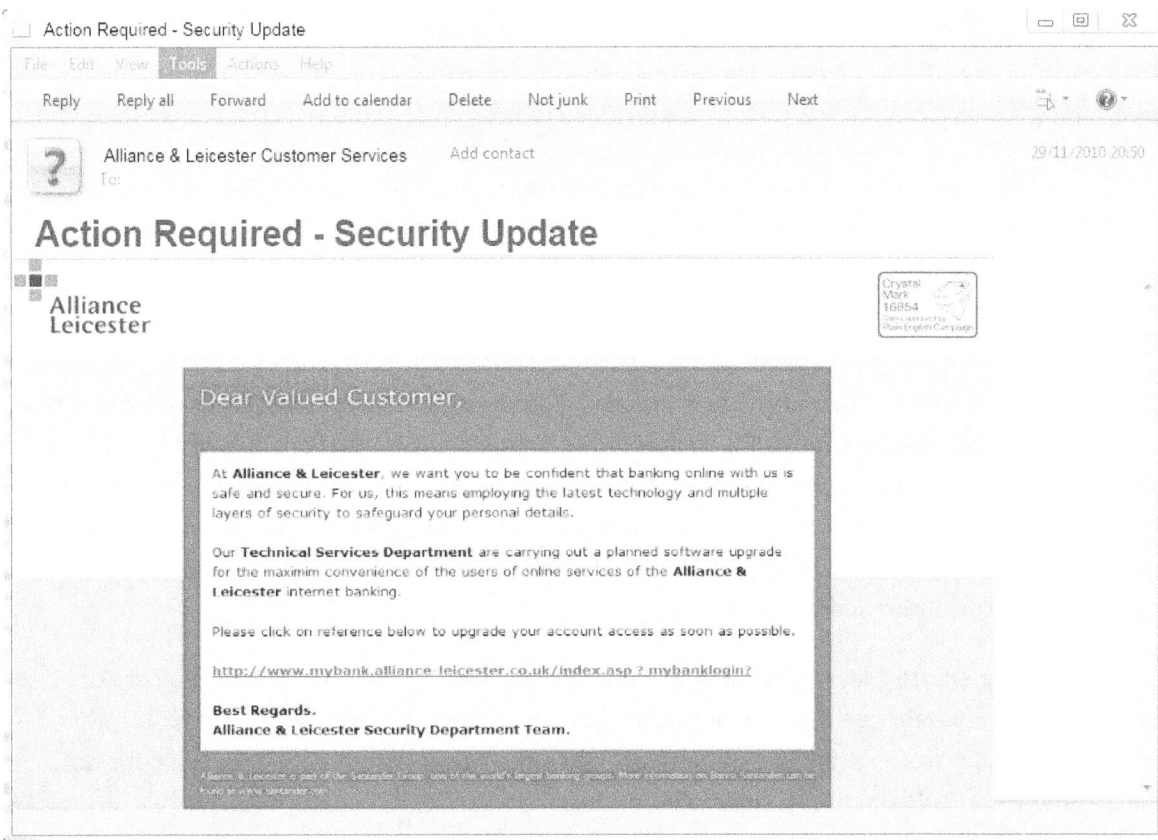

Clicking on the link, you are taken to a website that looks identical to your bank's website.

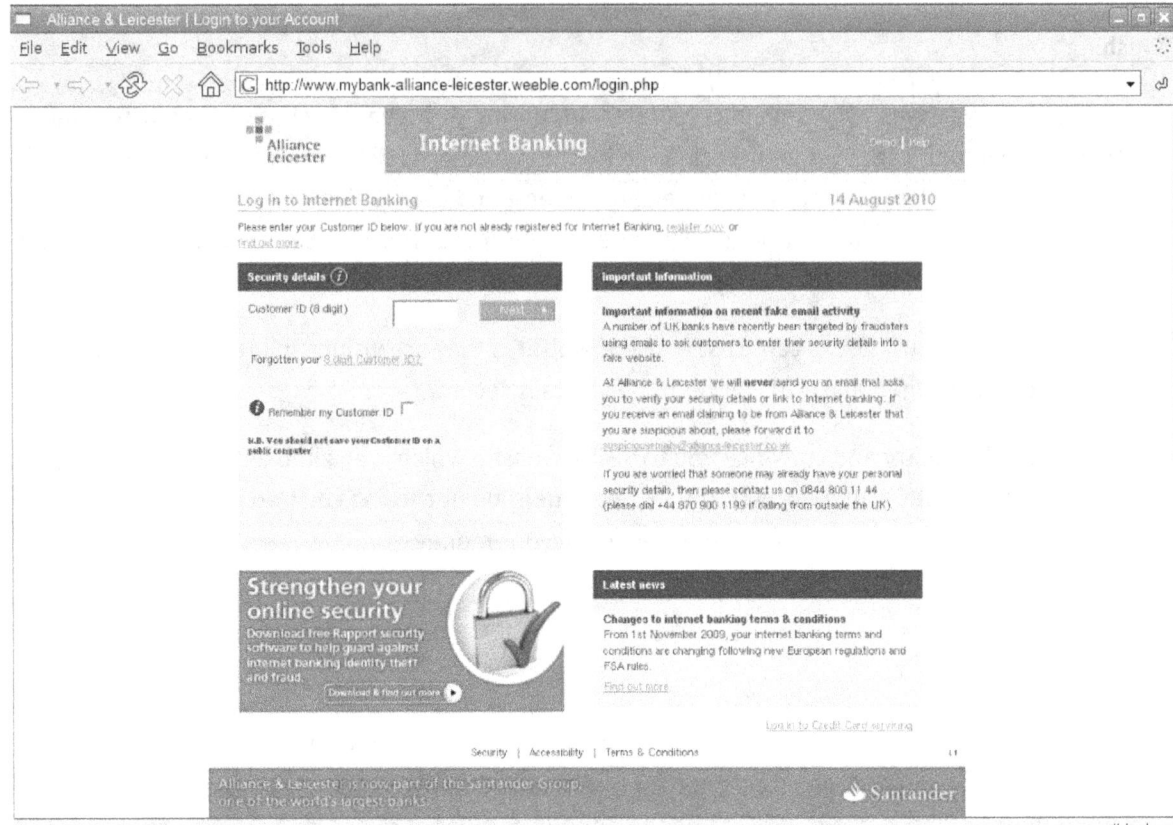

You enter your Customer ID, password and security information and log in as you would normally. You've just given all of your security details to a hacker who has everything he needs to access your bank account, transfer all of your cash to an anonymous offshore account and run up your overdraft to it's limit.

It's not just bank accounts that are targetted by phishing scams. You may receive similar emails from credit card issuers, online payment processors such as Paypal, Western Union or Moneybookers, auction websites like Ebay or even social media sites such as Facebook or Twitter.

How can you protect your business from this type of scam?

The latest versions of most web browsers include a "phishing filter" to protect you against this type of attack, but again they are not 100% foolproof. You should ensure that anyone within your Company who has access to online banking facilities are aware of the existence of this type of scam and are trained to never click on links in emails that purport to come from any organisation with whom you have a financial relationship. Instead, they should open their web browser and type in the official bank website address printed on your statements.

You should also ensure that whenever you enter your login details for any website, you are on a secure, encrypted webpage. This can be checked by looking at the web address in your browser's address bar. If it starts with the letters "https://" then the site is encrypted. If it doesn't, it's not secure and you shouldn't enter your details.

HMRC "Phishing"

Fantastic news! HMRC have checked your records and you're due a tax refund!

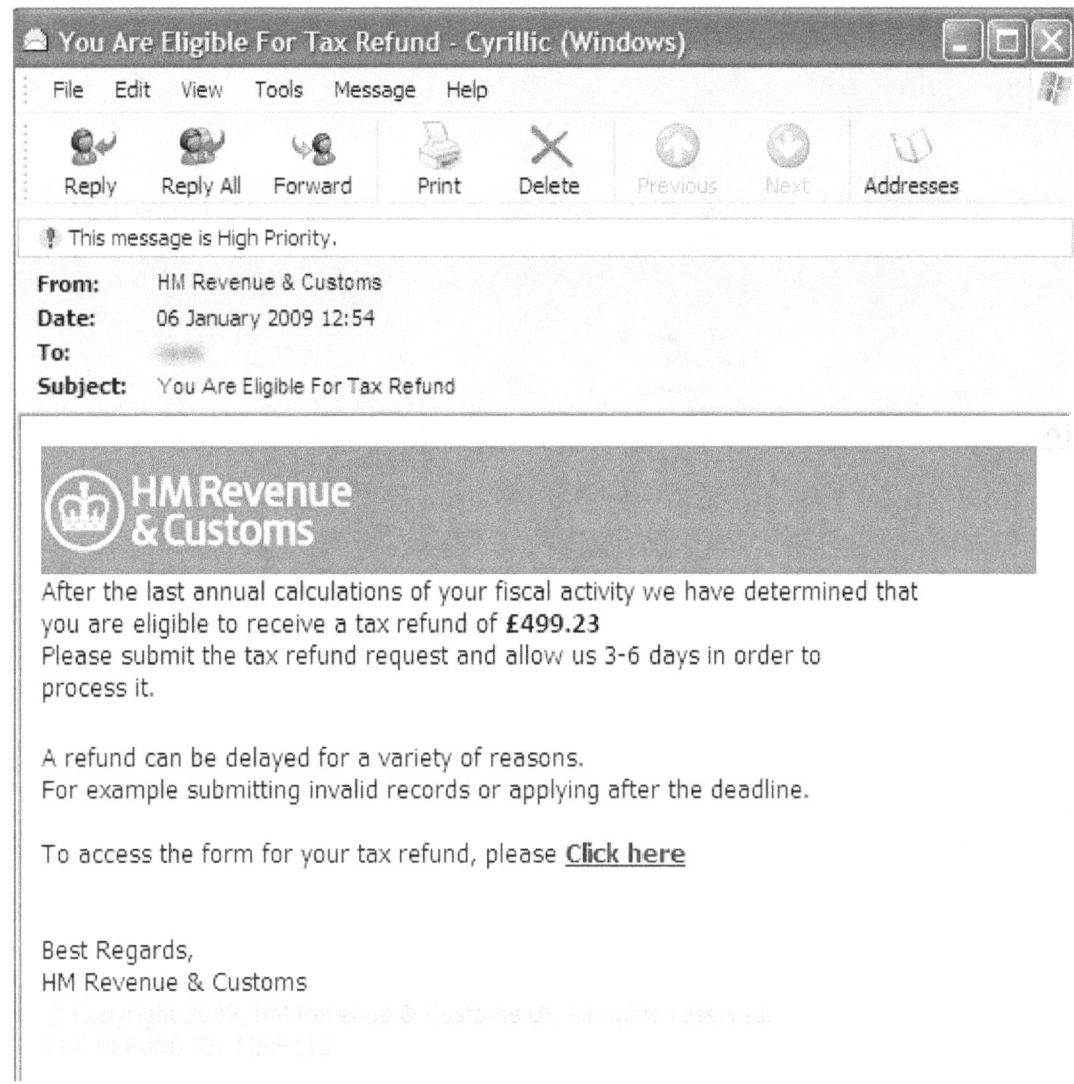

The email looks impressive and very official. It has the HMRC logo, copyright notice at the bottom and even an official Tax Refund ID code. The "From" field says that the email has come from HM Revenue and Customs and the email even tells you to expect a delay in receiving your money.

Everyone knows that the Taxman doesn't do anything quickly, especially if it's them owing you!

You click on the link to visit the refund application form secure in the knowledge that if it was a scam, they'd be asking for money, not offering it.

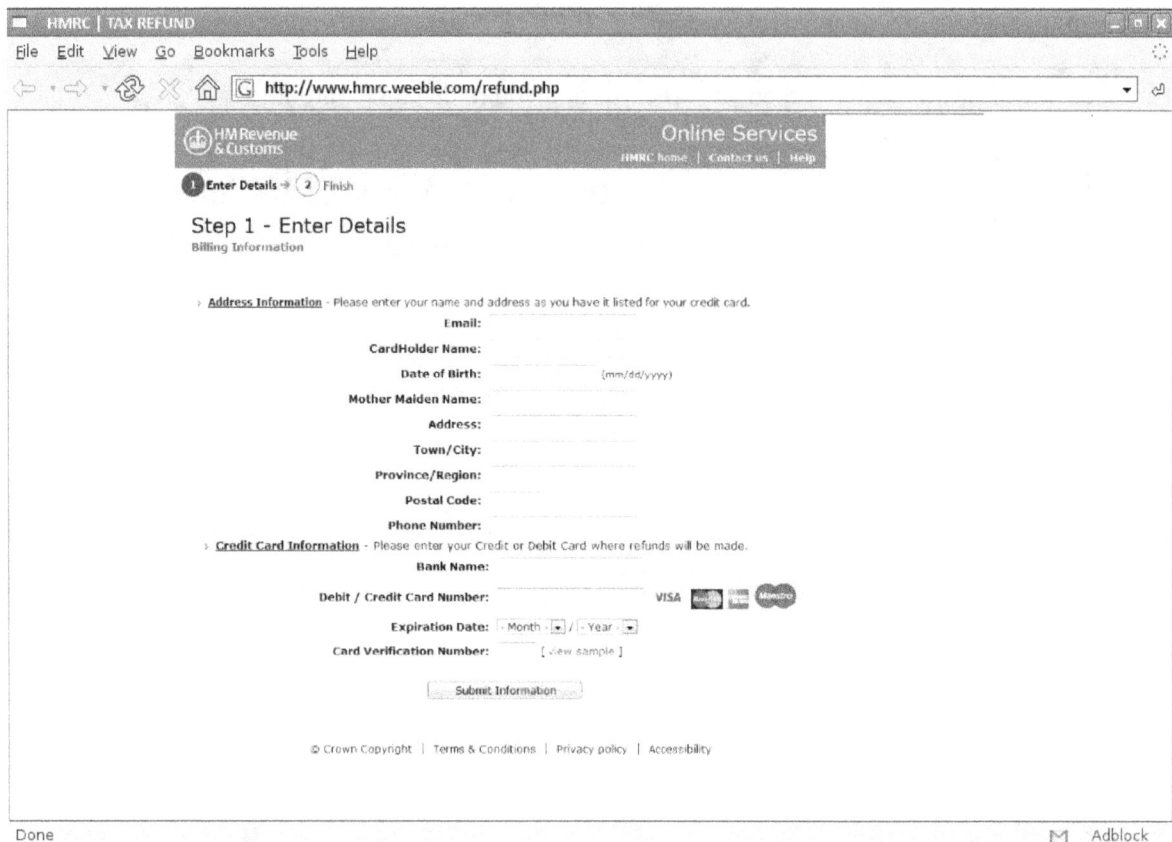

The website looks just as official as the email did. It has links to other parts of the HMRC website, a privacy policy and an accessibility statement, so you have no reason to think it's anything other than what is says it is.

You enter your card details, hit "submit" and wait for your refund.

Unfortunately, this is another variant on the "phishing" scam. Instead of going after your bank login details, these scammers have gone straight for your credit card number.

Rather than receiving your promised tax rebate, your credit card is now being used to buy expensive gadgets from online shops all over the world and you're going to get the bill.

The official HMRC website has this advice for Internet users worried about fraudulent emails:

HM Revenue & Customs (HMRC) do not send notifications of a tax rebate over email, or request that you update your security certification.

If you receive an email that doesn't address you by your first name and surname and then asks you to click on a link and/or disclose your details, you may well be revealing your details to a fraudulent website.

If you have received an email from HMRC that you consider to be fraudulent, please forward it to phishing@hmrc.gsi.gov.uk. HMRC cannot reply to every email, but action is taken on each report received.

More viruses and malware

We looked earlier at the threat of viruses and malware being installed on your computer by posing as funny videos or photos on social media websites. Another way your computer can be infected is through email.

Email attachments

A common method of getting you to inadvertently install a virus on your computer is by convincing you to open a file or document attached to an email. Often these emails will be similar to the "phishing" scam in as much as they will pose as a genuine organisation that you may have dealings with.

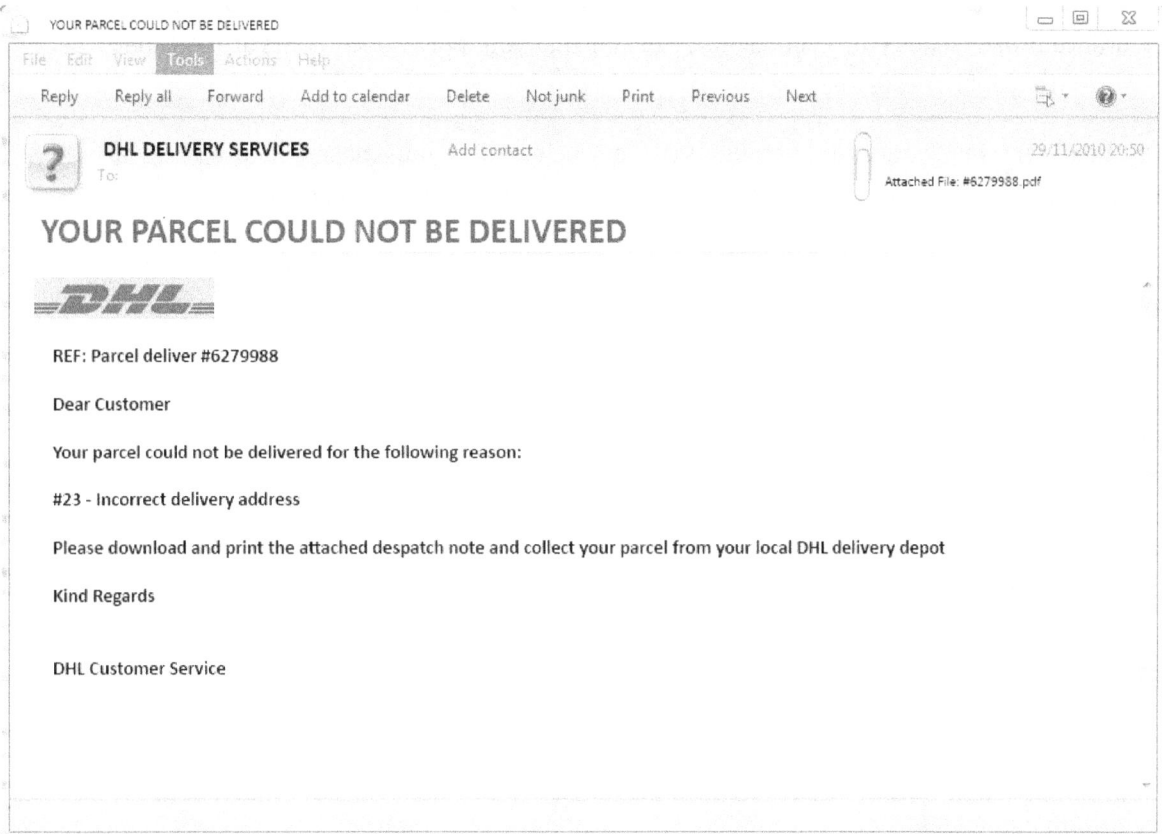

This email appears to come from parcel courier DHL.

The attachment in this case is actually a virus called infostealer. What this virus does is to trawl your computer looking for stored login details for the websites you use, including your online banking sites, sending them back to the virus creator so they can use them to steal your money.

If you receive an email like this, you should not open the attachment. If you think it may be genuine, you should call your local DHL office, getting the number from the official website or Yellow Pages. If there really is a parcel that needs to be delivered, they'll be able to tell you and will reschedule delivery.

You may also receive emails with attachments that promise sexy pictures of celebrities, the CV of a potential job candidate or a seemingly harmless screensaver or joke powerpoint presentation. They may come from a complete stranger, but remember that viruses will also send themselves to everyone in your email address book, so they could come from a trusted friend, supplier, client or colleague.

How can you protect yourself from email viruses?

The most important thing is to keep your anti-virus software up to date. However, as we've said before, no anti-virus solution is 100% foolproof so you need to train your staff to only open email attachments if they are absolutely sure that the person sending the email intended to send it.

A key indicator that the attachment is genuine can usually be found in the body of the email. If your insurance broker sends you an email that explains that your policy documents are attached, the chances are you'll be safe opening it.

On the other hand, would your number one client be emailing you a naked picture of Anna Kournikova? It's doubtful, and you should delete the email without opening it.

If in doubt, they should contact the person who sent the email to check that the attachment is genuine.

Other ways that viruses and malware can infect your computer.

Illegal downloads

There are literally thousands of websites offering access to the latest movies, music, software and video games for free. Usually utilising so called "peer to peer" technology, these website skirt around copyright law by not hosting the files themselves, offering only the software required for members to share media by making it available to other users from special folders on their computer.

Apart from the risk of exposing your Company to civil and criminal liability for unlawfully downloading copyrighted material, these sites can also harbour viruses and malware which could infect your computer.

Infected websites

Poor security measures can result in a website being compromised by hackers, thus becoming infected with viruses. Once infected, the website will initiate a download of the virus as soon as you visit it, without your knowledge and without you having to do anything at all.

Most anti-virus packages are very good at picking up these sites and block access before any harm is done, but you should exercise caution. Make sure you're using the most up to date version of your chosen web browser to stop websites installing software without you knowing and use a "pop up blocker" to stop websites from opening new windows without your consent.

Now you know some of the ways that your staff could accidentally install undesirable stuff on your computers, it's time to look at social engineering scams that could lead to you losing a fortune....

The Long Con

In this chapter we're going to look at how scammers can use email and the Internet to part you from your money.

As awareness of online scams grows, the perpetrators of these crimes have become increasingly sophisticated in their approach. They will use any means to convince you that their story is genuine, including fake websites, forged documents and stolen identities, in some cases even posing as law enforcement officials from the FBI and CID.

Perhaps the best known email scam is **Advance Fee Fraud.**

Also known as '419' scams (after the section of the Nigerian penal code that deals with"obtaining property by false pretences"), Advance Fee Fraud takes many forms, all with the same aim, to part you with your money. They don't just target little old ladies and it's not just little old ladies that fall victim. In fact, most victims of advance fee fraud are successful business people in their 40's and 50's who have made their money by not being too risk averse (and often by 'bending' the odd rule here and there).

The elaborate stories woven by the scammers vary widely, from deposed Nigerian Princes needing to hide their inheritance from a corrupt government to dying widows who want you to donate all of their late husband's fortune to charitable causes. The email may imply or state outright that the enterprise with which you are being asked to get involve is illegal (or at the least questionable) or it may sound like you're helping someone out who has been forced into a position whereby they have no option but to put all of their trust in a complete stranger. Whatever the tale, these scams all have several themes in common:

---

1) The sender has access to several million pounds/dollars but they need help to move it out of their country for some reason.

2) They need a 'trusted partner' to help them invest the money, using your bank account.

3) They are prepared to pay you a percentage of the total fund for your assistance

---

How does it work?

Imagine that you are a self-employed property developer. You have a small portfolio of houses and flats that you rent out to private tenants, along with your own website and 'blog' which attracts a modest amount of visitors. You're also working with a syndicate to build a small estate of executive houses and you're handling all of the payments to the contractors.

You're active on Twitter, Facebook and specialist forums for other property developers and because of your online presence you're often approached for advice on prudent investments and offered opportunities to buy land/property that could form part of your portfolio.

Because of the global nature of the Internet, these enquiries often come from people outside of the UK so when you start up your computer and find this message from South Africa you're not altogether surprised, although your eyes light up when you read the full content of the email.

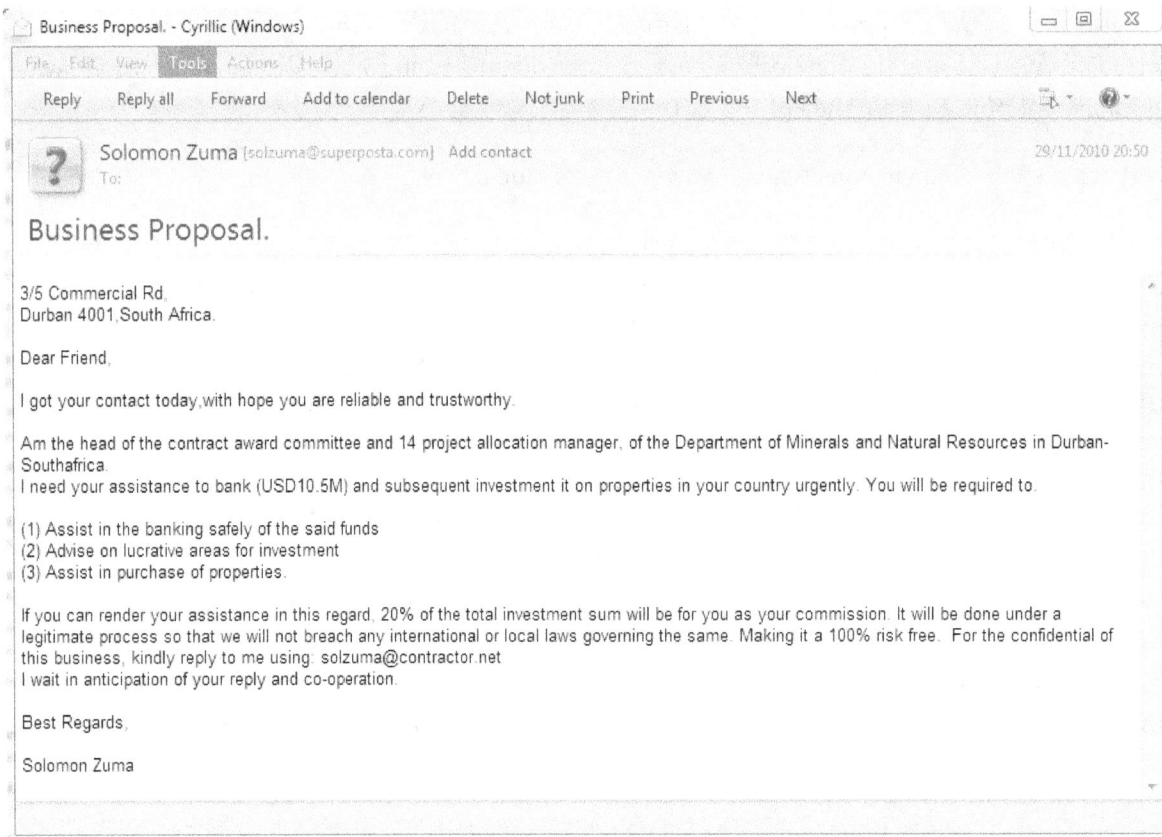

It sounds like a fantastic opportunity. A Government department in South Africa wants your help to invest over $10,000,000 in the UK, acting as their agent to find and purchase properties and your fee is going to be 20% of the investment.

You're excited! You've spent a lot of time building up contacts in the property business, so you're confident that you can identify the $10m worth of investment properties required by the contract and, let's face it, this could be opportunity you've been waiting for to make a name for yourself and catapult your Company into the big leagues.

You've heard about email scams of course, but this isn't from some deposed Nigerian Prince or anything silly like that, he's a professional who needs your expertise. Even so, you do a bit of digging on the 'net and find that there is a Solomon Zuma working in the Department of Minerals and Natural Resources in Durban, which in turn is located at the address given on the email. That's fantastic news, the guy's on the level and is who he says he is.

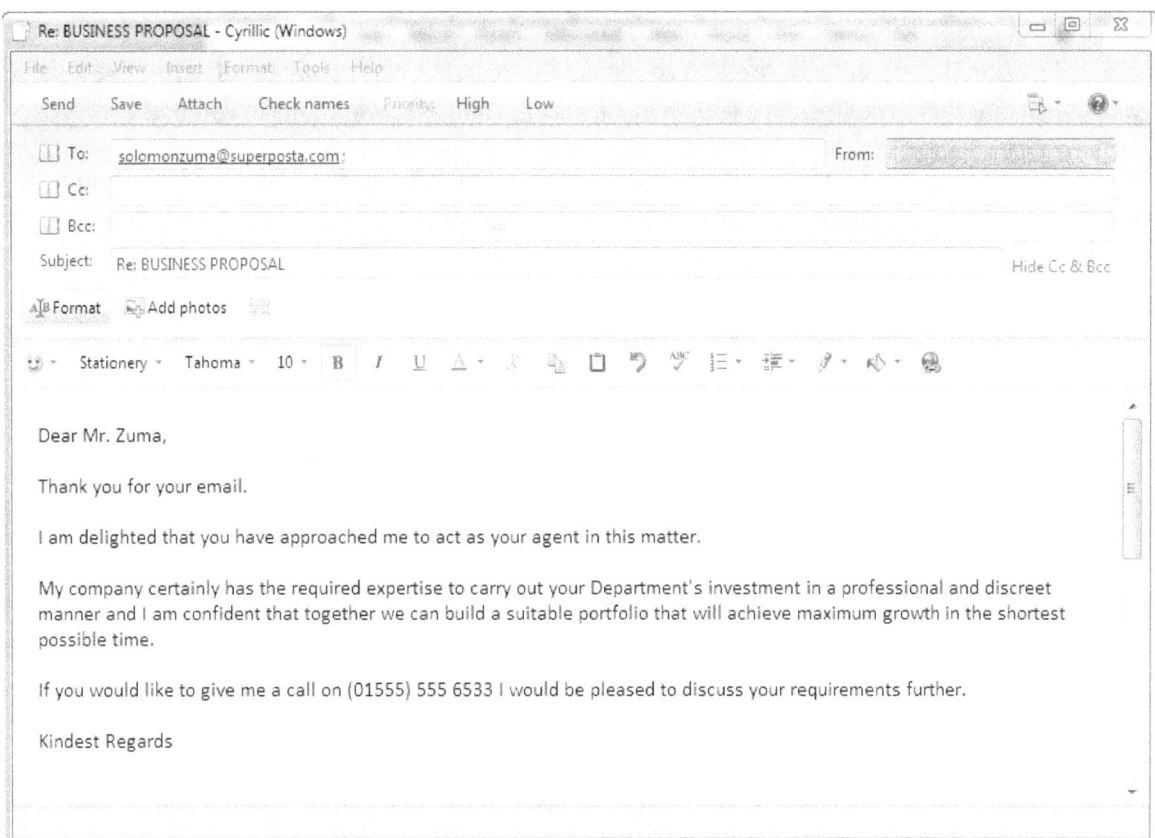

You respond to the email in a positive, professional manner and hit 'send', already dreaming of how you're going to spend the $2,000,000 commission. A new house? That sports car you've always dreamed of? How about a boat? Your wife's always wanted to go on a Caribbean cruise liner and your kids are always nagging at you to buy them the latest gadgets. They can have it all!

A few hours later the 'phone rings. It's Mr. Zuma and he explains that his Department has a cash surplus that has to be invested before the end of the financial year to protect next year's budget. Discretion is paramount because although the deal is totally above board and legal, there are 'political considerations' and he asks you to keep the deal under your hat. It sounds plausible and Mr. Zuma certainly seems to understand the property investment market. You spend a short time discussing details and verbally 'shake hands' on the deal.

Mr. Zuma ("please, call me Solomon") emails you a contract of services for your completion and requests a copy of your passport for his records and your bank account details so the fund can be transferred in the next few days. Because of the need for confidentiality, he doesn't want you to involve your solicitor, but the contract seems simple enough so you sign on the dotted line and send him all of the details he's asked for.

Now the deal's in writing you're getting really excited. You tell your wife that something big is in the pipeline but you can't talk about the details, but you give her your credit card and the latest holiday brochure and tell her to choose a cruise she likes the look of.

Early the next morning you check your email and find a message from a lawyer acting for the South African Government. He's identified a small problem. For the deal to go through, you have to be represented by a solicitor licensed to practice in South Africa. He can't represent you himself of course, because that would give rise to a conflict of interest, but he's happy to refer you to a trusted colleague in another firm. He gives you an email address and asks you to make contact.

Of course, you drop this solicitor an email immediately. He replies straight away and he's happy to take you on board as a client, but will need a small retainer. It's £500 and he asks that you use his "preferred payment processor", Western Union Money Transfer, to ensure that the payment reaches him immediately and avoid any delay in him starting work on your behalf.

Your local newsagent is a Western Union agent, so you pop round with the cash and send it to your new solicitor. You see a poster warning about sending money to people you don't know and it does cause you to pause for a second, but you're sure the lawyer is genuine, after all, he was recommended by the Government.

Your new lawyer emails you later that day to thank you for your payment and sends you a transfer document from the South African Reserve Bank to sign and return. It's an official looking form that has all of your details correctly completed and includes a tick box that says that the transfer will take a maximum of 48 hours from receipt of the transfer fee, which you assume will be paid by your contact Mr. Zuma .

Your South African lawyer emails you back to tell you he's received the transfer form but there's some confusion over who should pay the transfer fee. He's arguing on your behalf that it should be paid by the initiator of the transfer, but the Government are saying that it has to be paid by the recipient. He's having a meeting tomorrow to iron it out and will call you as soon as it's resolved.

In the meantime, your wife has not only booked the cruise, but she's bought an entire new wardrobe because she "can't go on a five star holiday looking like **this**." Your credit card's getting close to the limit, but you're not worried, you're 48 hours from having over $10m paid into your bank account and pocketing 20% commission.

Next morning your lawyer calls. You're going to have to pay the transfer fee, it's bank policy and there's no way around it. He'll pay it from his office account now, and would appreciate it if you could send him the cash by Western Union so he can replace it straight away.

You withdraw £2500 in cash from your savings account and make another trip to the newsagent with the Western Union transfer. This time the assistant asks you directly if you know the person you're sending the money to, because "there are a lot of scams going on". You've spoken to the lawyer on the phone, so you say "yes," you know the recipient.

You call your lawyer and tell him that you've paid the money. He seems worried and you ask him what's wrong. He tells you that he's had a call from the solicitor acting for the Government and there's a problem. They've forgotten to ask you for a fidelity bond, which is an insurance policy protecting their investment in the event of you or one of your staff stealing the money. They're insisting on this policy being in place before they will initiate the transfer and it has to be underwritten by their own insurers.

To insure the full $10.5m will cost £35,000 and you have to pay it for the policy to be valid. To apologise for their mistake and as a gesture of goodwill, the Government has agreed that you will be reimbursed for the full cost of the policy on top of your commission, which will reach your account in 2 days. He gives you the details of a bank account to pay the money in to and promises faithfully that this is the very last obstacle to getting the full amount paid to you.

You've already invested £3000 in this deal and you're not going to let it go. £35,000 is a huge amount of money, but you can raise it if you use some of the money from your executive housing estate project. The money's there to meet payroll at the end of the month but you'll definitely be able to pay it back before anyone notices.

You wire the money electronically, your lawyer confirms receipt and you sit back and wait for the money to roll in. Two days later there's no sign of it and you're starting to worry. At the end of the third day you call your lawyer but the 'phone number is unobtainable. You email him but it bounces back as undeliverable. You call your bank and ask them to check for a pending payment. There's nothing in the system. Frantically you scroll through the emails relating to the deal and call the lawyer acting for the Government. Again, the number is unobtainable. So is Mr. Zuma's phone.

You Google the main switchboard number for the Department of Minerals and Natural Resources and give them a call. The receptionist puts you through to Solomon Zuma but it very quickly becomes apparent that this isn't the same guy you spoke to last week, he's never heard of you or any investment project in the UK.

Panic rising, you dial the number for the local police. A Detective from the Electronic Crimes division comes round to take your statement and tells you that you've fallen victim to Advance Fee Fraud. The Solomon Zuma you were dealing with was an imposter, and your 'lawyer' just another member of the gang.

The police check out the account you wired the money to and find that it belongs to an innocent housewife who believed that she was working as a payment processor for a multinational company, she's already wired the money to her 'boss' in West Africa. There's no chance of getting the money back.

During the investigation, it comes to light that you took the £35,000 from the payroll account without proper authority. You are arrested and charged with embezzlement and whilst the judge takes pity on you for having fallen victim to a sophisticated scam, you're still sentenced to six months in prison and ordered to repay the money, which is taken from the proceeds of the sale of your house after your wife leaves you.

That's how Advance Fee Fraud works. A popular television drama repeatedly asserts that you "can't cheat an honest man" but frankly, that's rubbish. Often victims of this type of scam aren't greedy and gullible people out to make a dishonest fortune but genuine, honest business people just like you and me who believe that they are getting involved in a genuine business transaction in the Global marketplace.

This scenario sounds like a made-for-television movie but it's a true life story of a real victim. The victim, who wants to remain anonymous, said several times that he became suspicious of the transaction when the scammer started to ask him for money, but got so caught up in the excitement of it all that he let his 'heart rule his head' and carried on regardless.

Why do victims keep sending more and more money?

Have you ever invested money into a project that went over budget, but you'd put too much into it to pull out and risk losing your initial investment? That's called "Escalation of Commitment" and it's what the scammers rely on. They ask for relatively small amounts of money to start with, a drop in the ocean compared to the ultimate promised payout. The amounts then increase until the victim can't afford to stop sending money because they've already sent more than they can afford. Once they get to that point, the scammers go for the big score and ask for a much larger amount knowing that the victim will try and raise the money because it's the only way they're going to get back what they've already laid out.

The Recovery Scam

Just for a moment, let's put you back into the shoes of our property developer from the last segment.

Six months later, you're out of prison and trying to get your life back to where it was before you heard of Solomon Zuma. You managed to keep hold of a couple of your properties through the divorce and they bring in a bit of rent, but your reputation in the business is shot. One morning you open up your email inbox and find this message:

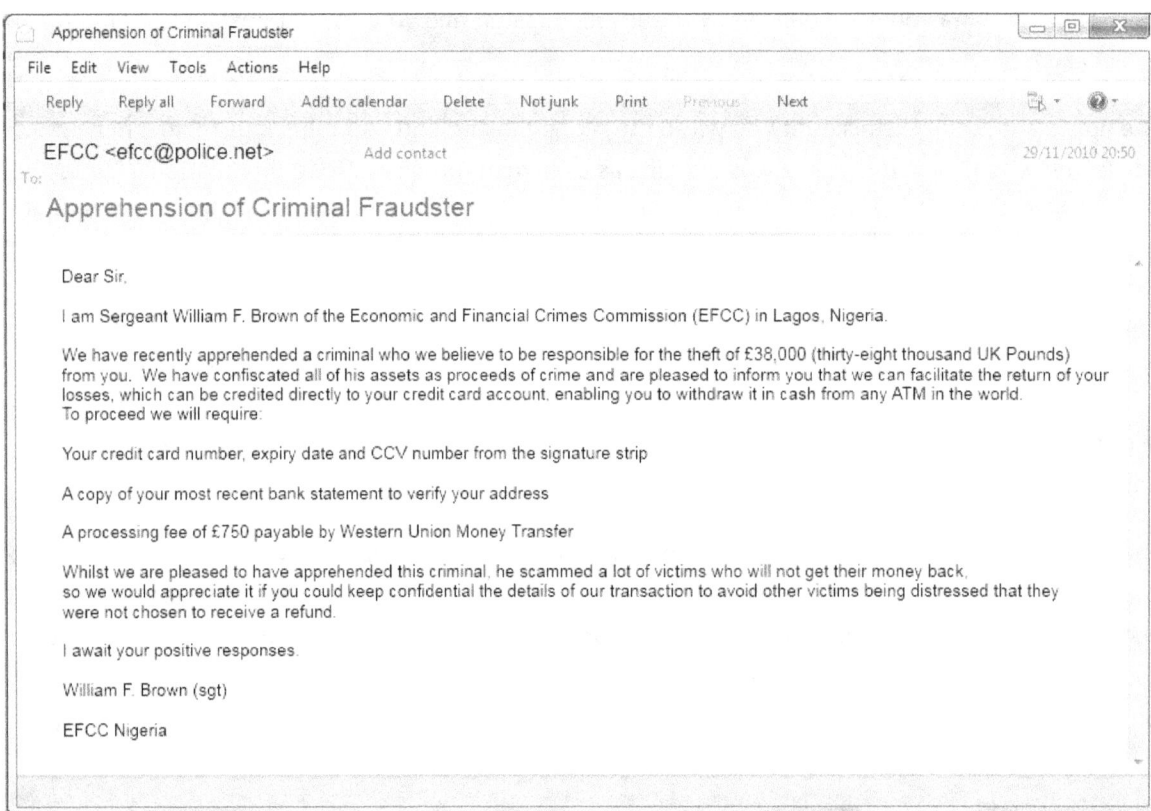

You've already paid back the £35,000 you took from the payroll account, and done your time for the embezzlement so if you can get the money back from the scammers then it's yours free and clear. £38,000 would go a long way towards a deposit on your next investment property and you could start to build up your portfolio again. The Electronic Crimes division of your local police force had mentioned the EFCC during their investigation so you know that they are the law enforcement agency that deals with Nigerian scams. You can just about scrape together the £750 and it's a small price to pay to get your money back.

To cut a long story short, your credit card is maxed out within hours of your return email and your £750 is gone. The email was from the same gang of scammers that put you in prison all those months before. They've played on the one weakness you have left, the desire to get your money back and they've taken you in again. Feeling stupid and gullible, you don't even report it this time.

You manage to convince your credit card issuer that you've been a victim of fraud and they cancel the balance on your card; you try and put the whole sorry experience behind you.

Unfortunately, your experience with the scammers still isn't over.

A month later you receive the first loan statement. It's from a Company you've never heard of and it says you owe £5,000 on a three year loan. You call them and they're adamant that you borrowed the money. They have your passport and a recent bank statement on file as proof of ID and the signature on the form looks just like yours. Then you get a mobile phone bill with a £300 balance. A missed payment reminder from a car finance company follows, along with a couple more loan statements.

Just when you thought it couldn't get any worse, the penny drops. The scammers have used the documents you sent them to steal your identity and apply for thousands of pounds of credit. Your credit rating is worse than it's ever been and the bank has foreclosed on your overdraft.

You contact the credit reference agencies and flag all of the suspect accounts that appear on your credit reports. They put a fraud marker on your account to stop any more accounts being opened but this means that your access to credit is virtually zero.

It takes months to sort it all out and get your credit score back to where it was and you've spent literally hundreds of hours writing letters and making phone calls to lenders to explain that you've been a victim of identity theft.

To protect yourself from this kind of scam ask yourself:

- Is the scenario being described in the email likely or probable? In this instance, would a representative of a foreign Government approach a small property developer by email to help with a multi-million dollar investment?

- Why are they approaching you? Are you qualified or experienced enough to carry out the investment required? Would the organisation need to pay someone such a large amount of money to carry out the project, or could they just use someone they already employ?

- How did they get your email address? Would someone you know have referred you to the organisation? Has anyone told you to expect a referral? Are you well enough known in your field for them to have sought you out in particular?

- Why is the organisation requesting payment by Western Union or Moneygram? A genuine business/lawyer/bank would accept BACS or SWIFT payments internationally. They would have no need for Western Union, chosen by scammers because once cashed, payments are untraceable.

- Is the deal too good to be true?

No matter how good the opportunity seems, how much money it promises or how much you're tempted by the prospect of a big deal, you should delete the email without responding. Replying to the email, even if it's to tell the scammer exactly what you think of him, will only confirm that your email address is live and leave you open to receiving more scam emails.

The Stranded Traveller

How does it work?

You receive an email from an old friend. It addresses you by name and spins a sorry tale of a friend in need.

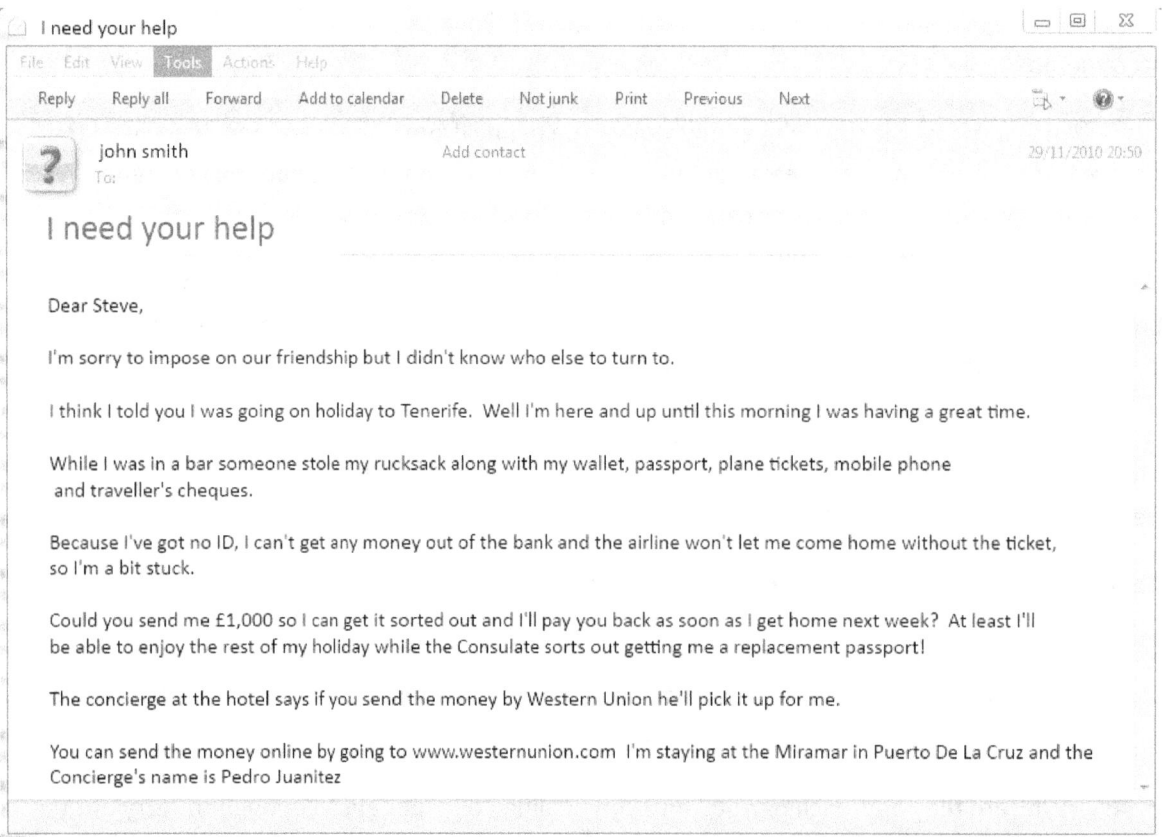

It's a plausible story and your heart goes out to John. After all, it could happen to anyone and you'd hope that if you were in the same situation one of your friends would do the same for you. You happen to know that John went through a nasty divorce last year and his ex-wife wouldn't spare him a bucket of water if he was on fire. You also know that his parents aren't well off so it really seems as though he has nobody else to turn to.

You visit the Western Union website and send the money.

A week later you phone John to check that he got home safely. He's utterly confused because he's still on holiday in Tenerife but hasn't lost his wallet, credit cards or passport and he's having a great time. He hasn't sent you any email and isn't in any trouble at all.

You've been ripped off to the tune of £1,000 along with four more of John's friends who also took pity on him and sent money to help him out.

So what happened?

John's a bit of a workaholic, and he travels a lot, so he uses a web-based Hotmail account to keep track of his email wherever he is in the world. Even though he was on holiday, he couldn't resist popping into a cybercafe and checking his email to make sure everything was OK at home.

Unfortunately, he forgot to click "log out" when he'd finished checking his messages, so the next person to use that particular computer was able to go straight into his account without needing a password. As it happens, the next user was a local criminal who spent a lot of time in the cafe watching out for tourists making exactly that mistake.

The scammer went through all of John's email contacts, sending the same sob story to all of them in the hope that at least one of them would be a good Samaritan who would happily help out a friend in need.

How can you protect yourself from this scam?

Don't take emails at face value. If a friend contacts you with a plea for help you should use an alternative method to contact them to verify their story. Don't reply to the email, because your message will be intercepted by the scammer. Call their mobile phone, or the hotel they're claiming to be staying at and speak to them directly. Above all, don't send any money unless you're 100% sure that the story is genuine.

Remember that one sure hallmark of a scam is the request to send money by Western Union, Moneygram or a similar wire transfer service.

These services are popular with scammers because it's almost instant and once the cash is picked up it's virtually impossible to trace. The relative anonymity is also attractive, because whilst most offices insist on some sort of ID, the scammers don't generally have any problem getting hold of fake credentials and there's no real address verification.

Because of the global network of Western Union outlets, the scammers can easily claim to be in, for example, London, Paris or Madrid, whilst actually collecting a payment in West Africa, Holland, Australia or even the next village.

The wire transfer services do try and warn their customers about scams and ripoffs, especially where they see a large transfer going to one of the scam 'hotspots' and have issued this advice to customers:

- Never send money to a stranger using a money transfer service.

- Beware of deals or opportunities that seem too good to be true.
- Don't use money transfer services to pay for things like online auction purchases.
- Never send money to pay for taxes or fees on foreign lottery winnings.
- Never send a money transfer in the name of a friend or relative with the intention of changing the name to someone you have not met personally.

The fake purchase order:

How does it work?

You receive an email from a trusted client placing a large order for collection.

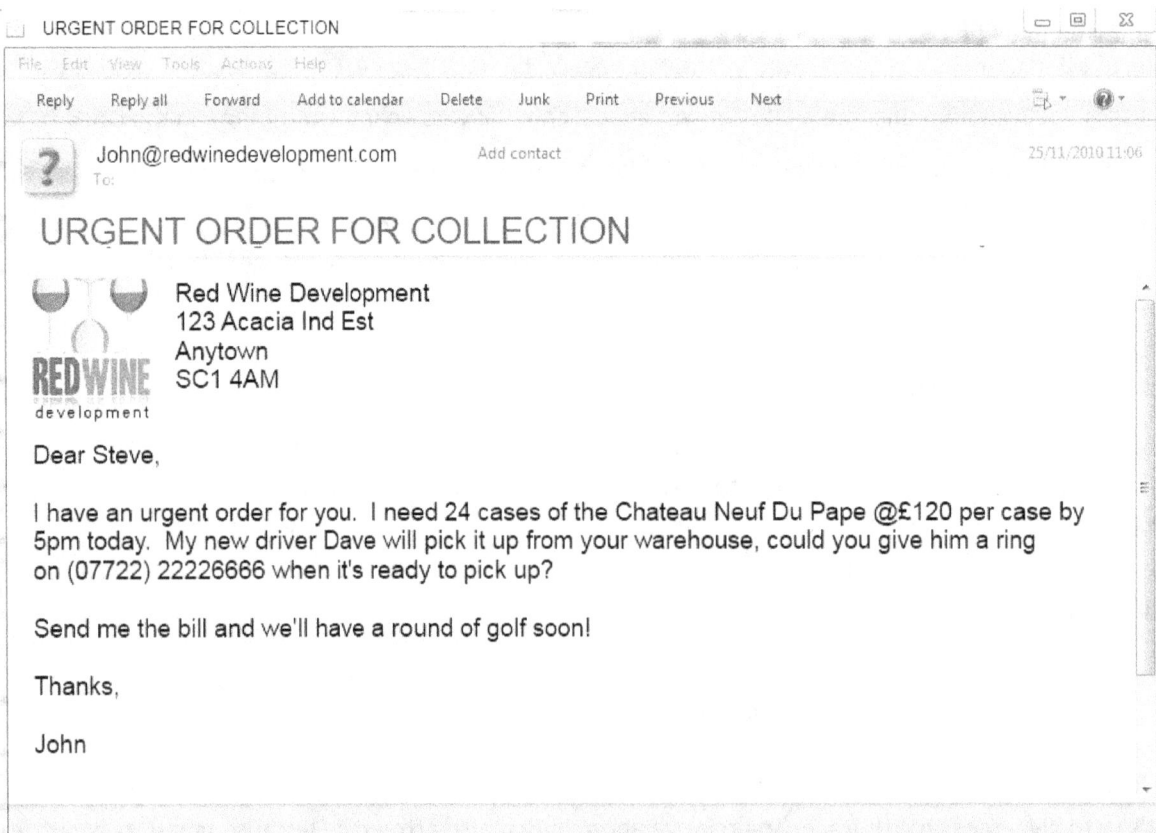

It comes from the client's email address and has their logo on it. It addresses you by name and the sender even knows to sweeten the deal by inviting you for a game of golf.

You prepare the order as requested and ring Dave the driver to come and pick up the consignment. He turns up as planned and everything's fine. You pass the signed collection note to the accounts department and the invoice goes to the client as normal.

Two days later and the client's on the phone querying the invoice. They don't have a driver called Dave and they don't know anything at all about an urgent order.

You're nearly £3,000 of stock down and the worst thing is, you helped Dave load the van personally.

So what happened?

Similar to the stranded traveller scam, this is the result of a compromised email account. By hacking into the client's email system, the scammer has been able to find out what suppliers they use regularly, who the named contacts are and what size of order is likely to be accepted without raising any eyebrows.

Once he identified your Company as the target he was able to rifle through any emails between you and the client to pick up on a little detail (such as the offer of a game of golf) that would further convince you of the authenticity of the order.

By including the driver's mobile number the scammer reduces the chance of you calling the client to confirm the order, and of course if you'd replied to the email he'd have been able to intercept it before it got to the client.

Of course, it's the client's responsibility to ensure that their email system is secure and you could insist that they pay for the order in full, but they're one of your best clients and if you make them pay you'll probably lose their business forever.

How can you protect your business from this type of scam?

Don't take email at face value . Insist that your staff call to confirm EVERY order received by email using the landline number on the client's file. Do not release goods until the order has been confirmed verbally. If you explain to your clients that this is to protect them from fraudulent orders being placed on their account they'll understand.

Overpayment scams

How does it work?

You receive an order from a new overseas customer, who agrees to pay your invoice in advance by cheque. You're happy because it's quite a big order and the client has promised to by a similar quantity of products every month for the next year. He's arranged for the goods to be transported by ship so he only needs you to deliver the goods to a storage warehouse at the docks.

When the cheque arrives, it's made out for several hundred pounds more than the invoice amount. You call the client and he says that he's made a mistake by combining the amounts for your invoice and the shipping agent's fee.

He asks you if you could bank the cheque and send the difference to his shipping agent by wire transfer so that his mistake doesn't delay the transport of the goods. It sounds plausible and you want to please your new customer, so you bank the cheque.

You're not daft enough to ship the goods before the cheque clears, so you wait three days and as soon as the money's in your account you send out the consignment to the warehouse and send the money to the shipping agent by Western Union as requested.

A week later you get a call from your bank manager. The cheque has been identified as fraudulent and they have no choice but to recover the money from your account to return it to the rightful owner. He explains that they didn't know there was a problem until the account holder reported the money as missing when he got his bank statement, which is why it had seemed to clear into your account.

You've not only lost the goods (at a cost of several thousand pounds) but you're also down the thousand that you sent to the shipping agent. It's been an expensive week!

How can you protect yourself from scams of this nature?

If you are approached by any overseas client buying from you for the first time, you should ensure that you get references from other UK Companies that he has done business with, and that any payments are made from a recognised bank directly into your account.

If the customer must pay by cheque then you should ask your bank to verify the payment with the issuing bank before despatching any goods. Under no circumstances should you accept an overpayment. If the customer issues a cheque that is over the amount of your invoice, you should return it and ask him to reissue a cheque for the correct amount.

Domain Name scams

The 'brand protection' scam

How does it work?

Your Company's domain name is important to you. It's your brand on the Internet and to protect your brand identity you've bought the .com and .co.uk versions of your website address.

So when you receive an email advising you that a Company has tried to register your brand name with extensions like .biz, .net, .info and .org.uk you're naturally concerned. The email continues by telling you that the sales representative has run a check on the domain names and noticed your ownership of the .com/.co.uk extensions and wanted to give you the opportunity to register the other variants before releasing them to the client.

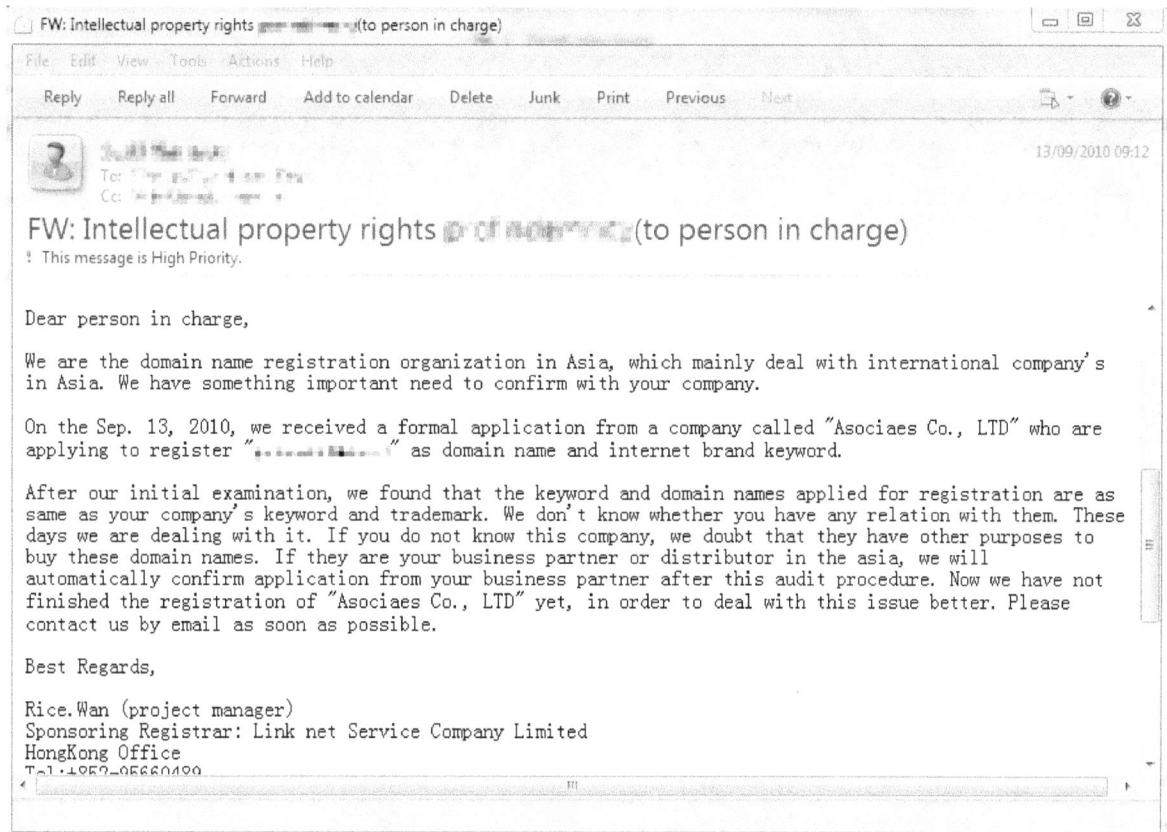

The representative will go on to offer the domains at vastly inflated prices, seeking to maximise their profit by extending the registration period from the usual two years to ten years, with the veiled threat that if you don't buy them, they'll allow this new firm to take them instead.

How can you protect your business from this scam?

Quite simply, delete the email and ignore it.

If someone wanted to register a variant of your domain name such as .net or .org and it was available, they'd just do it. The registration system is such that there's no human intervention and nobody could put a hold on the order while they check with other registrants that they don't want to buy the domains. They're sold on a first come, first served basis and if there's a dispute about rights being infringed later, then the lawyers will work it out.

Domain name renewal scams

When you buy a domain name, you do so through a company known as a "registrar". The domain name market is highly competitive and prices can vary considerably between suppliers, so it can be worthwhile shopping around, and it's common for website owners to transfer their domains to new registrars offering a better price.

Some unethical registrars will send out official looking emails to domain name owners informing them that their web address is coming to the end of the registration period and inviting them to click on a link to renew their domain online.

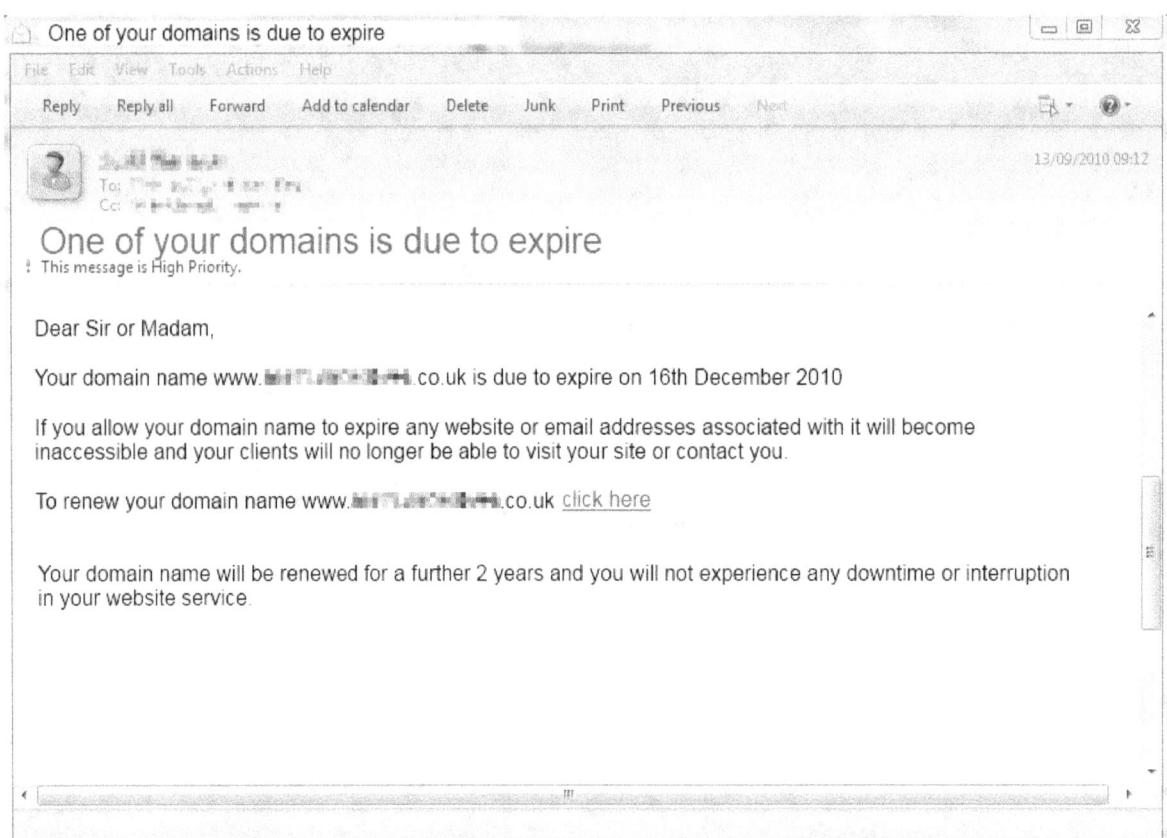

Clicking on the link will take you to a website where you will be charged an extortionate renewal fee of around £75.00 (which is ten times the going rate). Your domain name registration will be transferred to this new Company who will continue to charge you over the top rates and make it very difficult to transfer your domain back to your original supplier.

How can you protect your business from this scam?

Keep careful records of who you buy your domains from, how much you pay for them and when they are due for renewal. If you are in any doubt about a letter or email offering renewal, contact your supplier by telephone to confirm your renewal date and price.

The Professional Directory scam

Everybody wants to be recognised for their contribution to their chosen industry, so when you receive an email congratulating you on your nomination to be included in a Global directory of outstanding Professionals you're flattered. A committee of esteemed judges has chosen you to be included and your name and business profile will be included in a "who's who" of the great and the good throughout the world.

The email is full of compliments, describing you as a "leader in your field" and a "distinguished Professional" and promising that the directory is used as a daily reference tool by academics, journalists and other Professionals to find information about the "World's most experienced men and women".

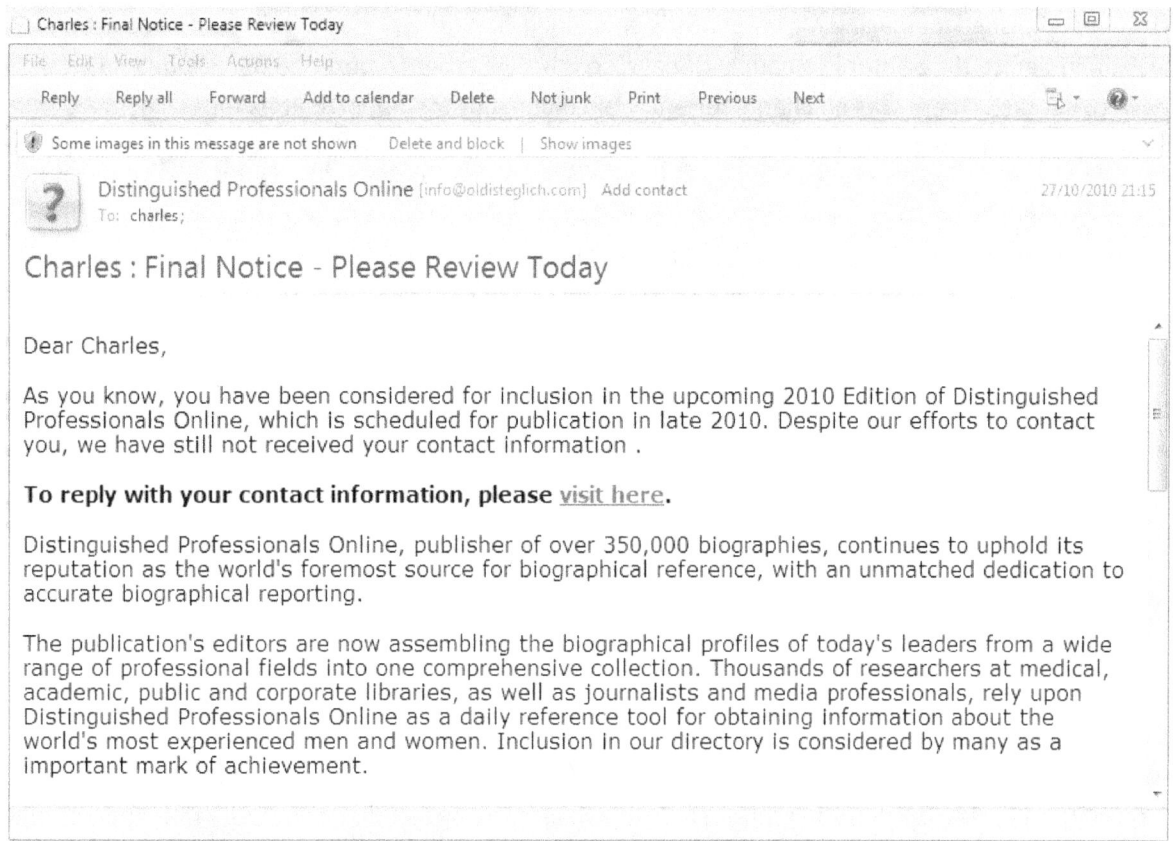

How does the scam work?

Although the email promises that entry into the directory is free, you will be expected to buy a copy of the directory to see your entry in print. Along with a certificate confirming your status as a "Distinguished Professional", this leather bound tome will cost you in the region of £400 - £700.

Just how choosy is the "selection committee"?

When I was "chosen" to appear in one of these directories, I decided to find out.

I submitted an application in the name of Mr. Casper LeSerpent, a specialist in the field of rodent control. I described his painstakingly environmentally friendly mouse disposal method , making use of neither unhygienic traps or potentially dangerous poison.

Within a week I received a telephone call from a researcher for the directory. Unfortunately, Mr LeSerpent wasn't available, but as his PA I was pleased to speak on his behalf.

The researcher spoke almost uninterrupted for around 20 minutes about how impressed the selection committee had been with Mr LeSerpent's methods and how his "significant reputation" within the industry had marked him out as an ideal candidate. Before Mr LeSerpent had even submitted his application the committee had received several recommendations from others within the rodent control industry suggesting his inclusion.

Once he'd finished massaging Mr LeSerpent's ego, along came the pressure selling. The directory was due to go to the printer in a couple of days, so if Mr LeSerpent wanted to be included he would have to act fast. There was no charge for entry of course, but the opportunities for business networking would be massive.

The publisher's experience showed that those included in the directory were 75% more likely to do business with other industry leaders listed in the directory than those who weren't, so buying a copy would give Mr LeSerpent access to business leads he would never have access to otherwise. To get his copy, all that was required was a payment of £650 by credit card.

Who is Casper LeSerpent? He's actually our family pet, a corn snake who eats a diet consisting exclusively of mice. His "rodent control" method? Constricting his meal before eating it.

Evidently there are no special requirements for inclusion in these directories. Anyone who can fill in a form online (or have someone do it for them) and can afford a few hundred pounds can be included, regardless of any achievement (or lack thereof) in their chosen field.

How can you protect yourself from this scam?

Don't let your ego rule your head. You're far more likely to get business by investing in a decent website and a search engine optimisation specialist to ensure that your Company is found by those looking for a Professional in your chosen industry than by being listed in a directory that appeals only to the vanity of those included within it.

The Data Protection Scam

Every business in the UK that holds personal data that could be used to identify a living person (including telephone call recording and CCTV footage) must be registered as a "data controller" with the Information Commissioner's Office to comply with the Data Protection Act. Fortunately, the registration process is simple and inexpensive, costing businesses with a turnover below £25.9m employing less than 250 staff only £35 per annum. Unfortunately, it's easy to forget to do this, and the penalties for not registering can be severe. That's why scammers have been able to use fear and ignorance of the law to get rich scamming business owners with the Data Protection Scam.

How does it work?

You receive a letter or email from a Company calling itself "Data Protection Services" or similar, advising that you have failed to register your business under the Data Protection Act.

The letter may warn of dire consequences for failing to register and impose a deadline for responses, and will offer to handle your registration in return for a fee of anything up to £250.

How can you protect yourself from this scam?

Businesses in the UK can check whether they need to register with the Information Commissioner's Office by completing the self-assessment questionnaire on the official website at **www.ico.gov.uk/**

If you do need to register you will be able to do so by completing a simple form and making your payment online.

Do not respond to letters or emails demanding payment for registration for statutory requirements without checking with the appropriate Government department first.

These are just some of the most common email scams that have been reported. As awareness of these schemes increases, scammers are constantly on the lookout for new angles and ruses to part you from your cash. The best weapon against the scammers is education and vigilance. Train your employees to question any approach by email, be it a purchase order from a client or an opportunity to pull off a massive deal with little or no effort. **If in doubt, check it out!**

Although email is by far the most common vehicle for scams and ripoffs, many scammers rely upon a silver tongue and persuasive sales technique to gain your confidence.

In the next chapter we'll explore a few of the ways that criminals may try and charm the money out of your wallet over the 'phone.

Telephone Scams

Technical Support Scams

"Good Afternoon Sir. My name is Roger and I'm calling on behalf of Microsoft. We've been advised that your computer has been infected with a Trojan horse and is spreading the virus to all of the contacts in your address book. We have developed a tool to remove the virus and repair the damage. All you need to do is to authorise me to access your computer remotely so I can install the fix. There'll be a small charge of £50 but you can pay that by credit card. If I could just take your details I can get started straight away."

How does the scam work?

This is a classic cold calling scam. The caller is not from Microsoft, or any firm working with their authority. He's a scammer and all he wants is your £50. In return, he'll either do nothing at all, or if he's particularly smart, he'll install a "back door" into your system to allow him to log in again later and steal your confidential data. The scammers use big names like Microsoft to give them an air of authority and make you believe you're dealing with a large corporation.

How to avoid it

Never allow anyone to access your computer remotely unless you have engaged them as an IT consultant and have a service contract in place, and certainly never as a result of a cold call.

Telephone Preference Service Scam

"Good morning, I'm Lisa and I'm calling from Telephone Preference Services. This is just a courtesy call to let you know about a new service to help you cut down on sales calls. We put your telephone number on our database and it removes your number from all of the marketing lists so Companies know that you don't want them to call you. Would you like to go on the database? You would? That's great. There's a small charge of £35 a year for business users, would you like to pay that by card?"

How does the scam work?

The Telephone Preference Service database does exist, but it's free to sign up for it and it's easier than handing over your credit card details! The scammers are simply charging you for a free service in the hope that you'll happily pay £35 to cut down on time wasting cold calls. They probably won't even register your number.

How to avoid it

If you're a sole trader or a partnership in England and Wales, you can sign up for the Telephone Preference Service online at **www.tpsonline.org.uk** . If you're a Limited Liability Partnership (LLP), Limited Company (Ltd) , a Public Limited Company (PLC) or any other form of corporate body including schools, Government departments or other public body, you should register with the Corporate Telephone Preference Service (CTPS) at **www.tpsonline.org.uk/ctps/what/**

SMS and Telephone Phishing

Although "Phishing" is primarily an email threat, there have been an increasing number of reports of mobile phone users receiving text messages asking them to call their bank to resolve a problem with their account.

 Upon dialling the number given, the user is then asked to speak their sort code, account number and password into an automated system so they can be 'directed to the most appropriate department'.

Alternatively you may receive a telephone call from "Customer Services" asking for the same information.

How does the scam work?

This is a more sophisticated version of email phishing. By asking you to call 'your bank' to resolve an account issue, the scammers remove the need to target a specific bank and therefore increase the response rate.

The automated system adds to the authenticity of the experience as many banks ask you to enter your account details before you speak to an adviser to save time.

When you enter your details, they are recorded by the system and sent on to the scammer, who can then access your bank account online.

In the event of a telephone call asking for security information, the scammer will simply ask you for all of your security information to verify your identity, for "data protection purposes".

How to protect yourself

As with traditional email phishing, the key is to not respond to this type of message. If you are contacted by anyone purporting to represent your bank and asking you to verify your security details, be it by email, SMS or telephone, you should not do so. You should hang up and call your bank's customer service department **using the number printed on your statement.** If there's a problem with your account, the representative will know about it and be able to resolve it with you over the phone.

The Mobile Phone Upgrade Scam

New regulations introduced in 2009 have reduced the occurrence of this scam, but it still goes on.

"Good morning, is that Mr xxxx? I'd just like to talk to you about your mobile phone contract for a moment. I'm calling from the upgrade department and I wanted to let you know that you can get a brand new phone for free. We're running a special offer at the moment too, you'll get a free Playstation 3 if you commit for two years instead of one. Would you like to go ahead with that sir?"

The next day a courier turns up with your new handset and a voucher to claim your free gift after 30 days. Two weeks later you receive two bills, one for your existing contract and one for a brand new contract that costs twice as much as the original one.

How does the scam work?

The phone call offering the 'upgrade' wasn't actually from your service provider, but from a reseller of their products and services. When you thought you were agreeing to upgrade your existing phone, they were actually signing you up to a brand new contract, which attracts a generous commission from the mobile phone network, hence the sweetener of a games console. By the time you get the bill, it's too late to return the phone because the network only allows a two week 'cooling off' period and you're stuck with a two year contract.

There have also been reports of dealers digitally editing recordings of the telephone call to completely change the nature of the conversation, with the edited version making it very clear that the customer is entering into a new contract and the customer's voice pasted into the conversation, answering "yes" when asked if they understand that they will be billed for a new line.

How can you avoid it?

Don't enter into binding contracts over the telephone. If you're looking for a new mobile phone, visit a reputable dealer and talk to a knowledgeable sales advisor about your requirements. Not only will they be able to identify the best deal for you (and give you any freebies that might be available) but they'll ensure that you get to keep your existing number and even transfer over your contacts list to your new phone.

Advertising Scam

"Hello, is that Mrs xxx? I'm calling on behalf of your local Police. We're publishing a child protection booklet to distribute to householders in your area to help them keep their kids safe. We're planning to send out 100,000 of these booklets but because of Government cutbacks in funding we can only do it if we can raise sponsorship from local businesses. You'll be showing your support for a really good cause, which will make your business look good, and your business name will be seen by 100,000 people too, which can only be good for you."

How does the scam work?

These Companies are hiding behind 'good causes' to raise your sympathy level and reduce your resistance to buying advertising over the phone.

As well as the "child protection" booklet, you may be asked to support calendars raising funds for a local hospice or children's home, wall planners supporting the emergency service or a diary being sold by a network of local charities.

Whatever the ruse, you can be sure that the majority of your money will be going into the publisher's pockets, with a tiny proportion, if any at all, going to the charity it's supposed to be supporting.

It's not unknown for the publication to never see the light of day at all, or if it does it's produced in nowhere near the quantities promised.

In extreme circumstances, the publisher will skip the telephone call altogether, opting to send you an invoice directly for the advert, despite the fact that you've never even spoken to them!

How to avoid it

Avoid agreeing to advertise in any publication that approaches you in this manner. If you want to support a charity, talk to them directly about the best way that you can donate. You may be able to sponsor a prize in a raffle or write an article for their newsletter or magazine. However you choose to donate, you'll present your business in a positive light and may even save a little on your tax bill.

The Boiler Room Scam

In this share dealing scam, you receive a phone call from an excited stockbroker who is offering you the opportunity of a lifetime to make some money in the City. There's a small, unlisted Company that's about to launch onto the stock exchange, or a technology stock that's about to explode. The broker may claim some inside knowledge about a report that's about to be issued, or a new product that's going to take the world by storm. Whatever the story, you have to move fast because the share prices are about to go through the roof and anyone in on the ground floor will make a fortune!

How does the scam work?

These scams work by creating a sense of urgency around an opportunity that won't be around tomorrow. Before they start calling victims, they'll have created a buzz on Internet forums, spreading thinly veiled rumours of something big in the pipeline, so if you Google the Company while their delivering their pitch you'll see some 'chatter' suggesting that investing now would be a good idea.

The stocks may actually be worthless 'penny stocks', be listed on an illiquid exchange and therefore virtually impossible to sell, or they may not even exist at all.

The 'broker' may use a grand sounding name and claim an impressive address in the City of London. In reality they will usually be based overseas, outside of the remit of the Financial Services Authority and once you've handed over your money they'll disappear altogether.

How to avoid it

Don't be tempted by a quick profit. If you want to invest in stocks and shares, use a reputable stockbroker who can demonstrate a track record of successful investment and knows what he's talking about. These scams can be highly lucrative for the scammers, with losses averaging £20,000 per victim, so remember that if a deal seems too good to be true, it usually is.

Other scams

Scammers are becoming more and more ingenious in their approaches and you may receive telephone calls, letters or emails that use stories that aren't covered here.

You should be aware that anyone who is offering a great prize or a once-in-a-lifetime opportunity to make a quick profit, asking you to support a good cause or warning of dire consequences if you don't comply with a registration requirement could be out to rip you off.

Don't commit to anything over the phone, stay cool and check out the organisation carefully before making any decisions, regardless of how "time sensitive" the offer may be.

Making your staff aware of these scams will help to prevent your Company falling victim to sophisticated fraudsters who will target your business.

In the next chapter you'll learn more about how scammers will use fraudulent websites to rip you off when you're buying goods or services online, or to convince you to send products to them before you've received payment.

Fake websites

It doesn't take long to build a website. With some technical skill and a few pounds for a domain name, you can have a convincing looking site up and running in a day or two. That's why it's so easy for scammers to use professional looking websites to support their scams and convince you that you're dealing with a genuine organisation.

This chapter deals with some of the scams that specifically target business owners and will help you to spot the dodgy sites that exist only to part you from your money.

Fake Escrow services

It's common for businesses to use an escrow service when buying and selling high value products and services. The escrow service acts as an intermediary between the parties, holding the payment from the client in trust, releasing it to the supplier once the client confirms that the product or service has been satisfactorily received or rendered. It's a useful way of ensuring that you get paid by a client you haven't dealt with before and can provide comfort and confidence to a new client.

Escrow is also commonly used when using online auction websites.

How do fake escrow services work?

The scammer will create a professional looking website that to all intents and purposes looks like a genuine escrow service provider. He will then place a large order for your products and suggest that for the protection of both parties, you should secure payment by using an escrow provider. Of course, he'll suggest the use of his "preferred service" and give you instructions to set up an account.

Once you've accepted the order, you'll receive an email from the fake escrow service advising you that your new client has made a payment which is being held pending confirmation of delivery.

You send the goods and wait for the money to arrive. It never reaches your account and you've lost your goods.

This method may also be used by a fraudulent seller suggesting that you pay the escrow service before they ship your goods. You pay the escrow Company but your goods never arrive.

How can you protect your business from this type of scam?

All escrow services in the UK must be authorised and regulated by the Financial Services Authority.

If a new client suggests the use of such a service, you should check with the FSA that it is registered with them. You can check the FSA register online at **http://www.fsa.gov.uk/register/home.do**

If it isn't registered, explain this to your client and insist on the use of a properly regulated service. If the client objects to this and continues to press you to use their "preferred service" walk away from the deal.

The fake courier scam

You agree to purchase a consignment of products from a supplier in the Far East. Because you haven't done business with them before, they suggest a method of staged payments to give you confidence that you will receive your goods.

You'll pay a deposit with your order, then they'll ship the goods using their "preferred courier", giving you a tracking number. Once you've verified that the goods are in the UK, you pay the second stage payment, at which point they'll authorise the courier to deliver the goods and you'll pay the final payment.

How does the scam work?

The scammer has set up a fake courier service website in advance, complete with a parcel tracking mechanism. Once you pay your deposit, he sends you the fake courier website address and the tracking number, along with an expected date of delivery of a few days from now.

On the agreed date, you check the website, enter your tracking number and confirm that the consignment is 'on hold' at a distribution centre close to your location. As agreed, you pay the second instalment.

At this point one of two things will happen. Either the scammer will break contact, or he'll tell you that you have to pay the final instalment before he'll authorise the release of the consignment. You've already paid two-thirds of the amount, so you can't afford to pull out, so you pay.

Either way, you'll never see the goods and your money's gone for good.

How can you avoid being ripped off?

Insist on the use of a well known International courier that you specify. A genuine supplier will not have an issue with this. If the supplier objects and continues to insist on the use of their "preferred courier" you should take your business to another seller.

The fake travel agent

Air travel is a highly competitive industry and prices can vary widely between the many different airlines operating around the World. Finding the best deal can be time consuming and frustrating when you find that the 'headline rate' doesn't include fuel subsidies, extra charges for luggage, check in charges, meals or even using the loo!

When you finally find a website that offers all inclusive flights with major airlines at fantastic rates, you jump at the chance! You buy your ticket, it's delivered by email and you even check the ticket number on the airline's website to make sure it's genuine.

Everything's fine until you turn up at the airport and find that the ticket has been cancelled. Not only are you not going to make that business meeting, but you're detained by airport security and interviewed by the police as a fraud suspect.

How does the scam work?

The tickets you bought were genuine. Your 'travel agent' has done everything he said he would and has booked the flights on your behalf. Unfortunately, he's taken your genuine credit card details, charged you the amount you agreed and then booked your tickets using a stolen card.

As soon as the transaction was flagged by the owner of the stolen card as suspect, the airline cancelled your ticket and put your name on the security watch list so you'd be detained as soon as you tried to check in.

By the time you've convinced the police that you're an innocent victim, your card has been used by the fraudster to book tickets ordered by other travellers.

How can you avoid this scam?

Only use recognised and reputable travel agents to make your flight arrangements. It may cost you a few extra pounds but you'll know that your tickets are genuine.

Business rate reduction scam

Every business is keen to reduce their ongoing overheads, so a website offering to reduce your annual business rate bill looks like a great opportunity. In return for an upfront fee they'll conduct a valuation of your property and lodge an appeal with the Valuation Office Agency. This, they claim, will guarantee a significant reduction in the amount of business rates you'll have to pay.

How does the scam work?

The website may simply take your money and do nothing at all in return, or they may send an unqualified 'surveyor' who will take your fee and add 'administration charges' that ensure that any reduction you do see in your rates is less than the fees you've paid. In some cases, their efforts can even result in an increase in your property's rateable value, with a corresponding rate increase.

How can you avoid being scammed?

Be wary of anyone who claims to be able to achieve a reduction in your business rates before knowing the full details of your property. Don't pay an upfront fee and make sure that the 'surveyor' is a member of the Royal Institute of Chartered Surveyors (RICS), the Institute of Revenues, Rating and Valuation (IRRV) or the Rating Surveyors Association (RSA).

Fake insurance brokers

Your Company spends a fortune on insurance to protect against claims of negligence brought by clients or suppliers, personal injury claims by employees or members of the public or claims as a result of traffic accidents. Some insurances are optional, but others are required by law or by your professional body before you can even open your doors.

The insurance market is very fluid and rates can vary wildly from year to year. A major catastrophe in one part of the world requiring massive payouts from insurers can result in Global premium increases for all policyholders.

Because of this variance in premiums between insurers, it can be a good idea to shop around for your insurances every year and many businesses use a specialist broker to secure the best deals.

Because you buy insurance "just in case" something happens, it's common for a Company never to have made a claim. As such, it's easy for a scammer to pose as a reputable broker and put together an all-inclusive package of policies that looks like it's going to save you hundreds of pounds, but will actually offer you no protection at all if you come to make a claim.

How does the scam work?

The scammer sets up a website and uses paid advertising to make sure it appears on the front page of the search engine results when you search for "business insurance" or a similar keyphrase.

When you visit the website, you're invited to get a quote online by filling in a form that asks for comprehensive details of your existing insurance policies and the premiums you pay. The website then produces a quote that undercuts your current provider by at least £500 and offers a further discount for upfront payment of the whole premium amount. It may even offer the facility to pay in interest-free instalments by standing order.

You pay the premium and receive your policy documents, which are delivered by email and look completely genuine, including policy numbers, claims helpline numbers and the logo of a well known insurance Company.

You file the documents and forget about them for another year, until something goes wrong and you have to make a claim. You call the claims helpline and find that your policy is a forgery. You're completely uninsured and have to meet the cost of the claim from your own pocket.

How to avoid being scammed

Every insurance broker in the UK should be authorised and regulated by the Financial Services Authority and provide their registration number on all correspondence, including on their website. You can check that your chosen broker is genuine by checking the FSA register online at **http://www.fsa.gov.uk/register/home.do**

The fake shop

Most businesses rely to a greater or lesser extent on the use of laptop and desktop computers, handheld devices and mobile phones in their day to day operation. These electronic goods can represent a significant investment and finding cheaper sources for these items can save your Company a lot of money.

Scammers know this and there are literally thousands of dodgy websites offering the latest gadgets at knockdown prices which will simply never be delivered.

Buying from these sites will at best result in you losing the purchase price. At worst you could find yourself falling victim to corporate identity theft and unauthorised charges to your Company credit card or bank account.

How to spot a fake shop

"Red flags" that may indicate that you're looking at a scam website include:

- **Unrealistically low prices** – 'too good to be true' deals are a sure sign of a scam

- **Payment options that include Western Union or Moneygram** (even if they also offer other payment options). Wire transfer service are popular with scammers because once the payment is made it's virtually impossible to trace the recipient.

- **No address or telephone number listed on the site** – The only method of contacting the website operator is via a contact form, online chat facility or free email address such as Hotmail or Yahoo.

- **A 'phone number that starts with 070, 071 or 072** – Whilst looking like genuine mobile numbers, these are actually "follow me" numbers that are charged at premium rates and can be redirected to any phone number in the World.

- **Impressive looking 'trust seals' that don't do anything when you click on them** - Trust seals are issued by third party organisations that verify the security and reliability of a website. They should always link through to a verification page provided by the seal issuer to verify their authenticity.

- **Protected "whois" data** – All website owners are registered on the publically available "whois" database. This should list the name, address and telephone number of the owner of the website. If this data is hidden by a privacy service, incomplete or contains fake information such as non-existent telephone numbers or addresses it's a sure sign of a scam.

- **No Company registration number** – If you're dealing with a genuine UK based Company they are required by law to state their Company registration number on their website. You can verify this number online by checking the Companies House database at **http://wck2.companieshouse.gov.uk** which will also tell you the registered office address of the Company and show how long it's been trading.

- **Copy that states that the business is "honest, legal, legitimate or real"** - No genuine business would state that they're not fake!

If any one of the above pointers applies to the website you're thinking of buying your PDA or smartphone from, you should be suspicious and check out the site further. Two or more and you've probably found a scam website and you should take your business elsewhere.

These are just some of the ways that scammers will use fake websites to gain your confidence and convince you to send them money for products and services that you will never receive. New variations on these scams are emerging every day and you should remember these golden rules whenever you consider doing business with anyone online.

1) If a deal seems too good to be true, it usually is

2) Before you hand over your credit card details, or accept an order where the client is insisting on unusual ways of doing business, check everything twice, then check it again!

3) NEVER pay for purchases using wire transfer services such as Western Union or Moneygram. No legitimate business is going to pay staff to drive to the agent's office, pick up the cash and then drive to the bank to pay in the money. The only reason for using these services is to anonymously pick up the cash without leaving a paper trail, so the scammer can't be traced when you don't get your goods.

In the next chapter we'll look at some methods you can use to protect your business against online threats and make your systems more secure.

Protecting your business

Now you know about some of the scams and threats that your business could fall victim to, it's time to look at how you can secure your systems and train your staff to reduce the chances of your systems being compromised or a fraudster getting one over on you or your employees.

Hardware solutions

Your first line of defence is technology. If your IT network is compromised by a hacker it could lead to a virus or "back door" being installed, giving the hacker access to your system and enabling the theft of your critical business data.

Firewalls

A firewall is effectively a security fence standing between your computers and the Internet.

Depending upon the complexity of your IT network, your firewall could be a separate piece of equipment connected to your server, or a software package running on your computer.

Regardless of which type of firewall you have, if it's properly configured it will control the flow of information both in and out of your network. For example, it may allow your web browser and email program to send and receive data via the Internet, but block instant messenger programs such as Windows Live Messenger to stop your staff from chatting with online friends when they should be working.

Spyware programs need to communicate with the Internet to send data to the hackers that are using them to collect information about your computer use. A firewall should stop this from happening and inform you that an unauthorised program is attempting to access the Internet.

A firewall will also block incoming connections to your network.   Hackers will use sophisticated technology to identify networks that are not adequately protected and exploit those vulnerabilities. Ensure that your firewall is configured to close down any open ports (access points for data connections) that are not required for your business activities.

IMPORTANT: Simply having a firewall is not enough. It must be properly configured to properly protect your IT infrastructure and you may need the assistance of a properly qualified IT security specialist to do this for you.

Uninterruptible Power Supply (UPS)

A UPS unit is effectively a rechargeable battery that will activate if the mains power is interrupted, enabling your system to continue to operate in the event of a power failure, giving you time to shut it down safely and reduce the risk of data loss.

Backup Solutions

You should install and use a secure backup solution to protect your critical data. Backup solutions may include portable hard drives, optical media such as CD ROM, DVD ROM or Blu-Ray disks or tape drives. Whichever solution you choose you should ensure that backups are made daily and the backup media is stored away from your business premises. If your business relies upon sensitive information such as credit card or bank details, or other identifiable client information your backup should be securely encrypted.

Removable media devices

Memory sticks and portable hard drives can be useful where employees are required to work on projects away from Company premises. Because they are small and easily misplaced, it's important that they are properly encrypted and secured by a password to prevent unauthorised access to the data contained on them in the event of loss or theft. There are a number of manufacturers who include encryption solutions as standard and you should insist that your staff only use devices which have been approved for use by the Company.

You should also be aware that some seemingly innocent electronic devices can double as portable hard drives and used to copy data from your computers. These include MP3 players, digital cameras and some mobile phones and you should be careful about authorising the use of these in the workplace if your data is particularly sensitive.

Hardware encryption

If your Company routinely handles particularly sensitive data, there are hardware encryption solutions available that require the use of a piece of equipment known as a "dongle", which is a separate device which plugs into your computer and ensures that without the "dongle" the data stored on the computer cannot be read.

Laptop Security

Data stored on Company laptops should be encrypted to secure against unauthorised access in the event of loss or theft. Staff who have been issued with laptops should also be issued with secure locking cables so that they can secure their laptop to an immovable object when it is in use, especially if it is likely to be used in public locations such as hotels, airports or on trains.

Software solutions

Software can also be used to help keep your system clear of viruses and malware and prevent unauthorised programs from connecting to the Internet.

Anti-virus solutions

There are literally dozens of anti-virus software packages commercially available, all with their own pros and cons. You should carefully compare the available systems to choose one that suits the complexity of your IT network. You should install a package that offers daily updates, as several thousand new viruses (and variants of older ones) are discovered every day. Some packages will only offer basic protection, whilst others will scan the websites you visit before they appear on your screen to ensure that it is safe to visit, check your email at server level (before it's downloaded to your computer) and monitor your system for any unauthorised programs attempting to send or receive data over the Internet.

Anti-Spyware programs

A good anti-spyware solution will scan downloads for known spyware, which can collate and send information about your computer usage to advertisers or malicious hackers. Some anti-virus solutions include this as standard, or you may need to install a separate package.

Advertising blockers

Some malicious website use paid adverts on search engines and other websites to convince users to click on the website. Ad blocking software will prevent these adverts from appearing.

Pop-up blockers

Some websites will surreptitiously open new windows in your web browser when you visit them. These "popups" are usually innocent advertising sites but can on occasion be malicious sites that will attempt to download software to your computer. The most up-to-date web browsers will block these popups automatically, but if you are running an older browser you may need to install a separate program or plugin to block them for you.

Operating system updates

As new vulnerabilities are identified, your operating system manufacturer (probably Microsoft) will release system updates to "plug the holes". You should ensure that your computer is set to download this updates automatically to ensure that your system is fully protected from the latest threats.

The human factor

Whilst technology can provide a first line of defence against Internet threats, they can't stop you falling victim to a scam, clicking on a suspect link or accidentally revealing system passwords and access codes. Staff training should be an important part of your IT security policy and the amount of time you dedicate to this will be dependent upon the complexity of your systems and the sensitivity of the data you handle.

Secure passwords

In December of 2009 the accounts of more than 32 million users of social networking website rockyou.com were accessed by a hacker and the passwords posted on the Internet.

A data security firm analysed this compromised data and released a top 10 list of the most common passwords.

They were:

1. **123456**

2. **12345**

3. **123456789**

4. **Password**

5. **iloveyou**

6. **princess**

7. **rockyou**

8. **1234567**

9. **12345678**

10. **abc123**

When you consider that another survey carried out during the same month revealed that over 50% of Internet users use the same password on multiple websites, it's easy to see why so many people fall victim to online hackers.

Your password security policy should put the onus on your employees to choose passwords that are not only unique but difficult for anyone else to crack. They should never use their name, date of birth, favourite football team, pets or children's names or any other information that would be common knowledge amongst co-workers or easily discernable from their Facebook profile.

A secure password will contain a mixture of upper and lower case letters, numbers and special characters such as !, £, $, % or *.

One way of devising a difficult to crack password is to think of a phrase that means something to you, such as "My favourite food is spaghetti bolognese."

Once you have your phrase, you should take the first letter of each word and put them all together, then add a random number at the end. Now you have "Mffisb21".

As a final touch you could subsitute letters for numbers, for example using a "1" instead of an "i". Now you have "Mff1sb21".

This is clearly a secure and difficult to guess password that would withstand most attempts to crack it.

Acceptable use policies

Strong acceptable use policies governing your employees' use of your IT systems can help to protect your system from the impact of data theft, loss and corruption as well as reducing the risk of breaches of confidentiality.

An effective IT policy will cover not only the use of the Internet and email, but also:

- Password management

- Removable media

- Health and Safety

- Remote access to your systems

- Working from home

- Mobile phones and handheld devices

- What your staff can (and can't) say about your business on social media websites

By including your IT policy statements in your staff handbook you can ensure that your staff are both aware of their responsibilities when using Company IT equipment and also the ramifications of neglecting those responsibilities either through blatant breaches of the policy (ie using Facebook during working hours or downloading illegal software, music and films) or through accidental exposure to viruses or malware caused by them disregarding the advice given.

Should it become necessary to discipline a member of staff over inappropriate IT use, the presence of a signed copy of the relevant IT policy statement in their personnel file will remove the defence of "I didn't know I wasn't supposed to do that".

Among many other things, your IT policy should forbid altogether:

Downloading unauthorised software

The downloading of unauthorised software (including free trials, shareware, games, screensavers, movies and music) could have multiple implications for your business. Not only could it infect your system with spyware, viruses or other unwanted programs, but, in the case of illegally obtained software, movies or music, it could leave you open to civil or criminal action for copyright theft.

Viewing pornography

According to adult website statistical analysts sextracker.com 70% of all online porn is viewed during working hours. This wastes valuable working time and could lead to claims of sexual harassment being made against workers if their colleagues catch a glimpse of inappropriate material when passing their terminal. Additionally, pornographic websites are amongst those most likely to be compromised by hackers, installing rogue diallers, spyware, viruses and other malicious software while the viewer's attention is clearly elsewhere.

Most organisations consider the viewing of pornographic material on Company IT equipment to be gross misconduct carrying the penalty of summary dismissal.

Connecting unauthorised devices to Company systems

Devices such as USB flash drives, MP3 players, smartphones and digital cameras can double as portable hard drives and are as susceptible to viruses and malware as any other computer. Simply connecting the device to charge it could be enough to enable it to transfer a virus onto your network. There is also the risk that these devices could be used to remove confidential data from your premises without authorisation.

Using personal social networking sites

We covered some of the risks that your staff could expose your systems to when using social media and networking websites like Facebook, Myspace and Twitter. Unless your staff need to use these sites to promote your business they should be discouraged (if not altogether forbidden) on Company equipment and during work time.

Scam Detectives has developed "The Complete IT Policy Toolkit" to help business owners develop a comprehensive IT policy for their business. You can find more information about the toolkit on **page 80**.

Staff training

Many Companies take on staff and allocate them a computer in the assumption that they know exactly what to do with it. Whilst most households now have a computer, many do not come with commercial packages such as Microsoft Office pre-installed and the experience of many people who claim to be "good with computers" is limited to buying and selling on Ebay, playing video games and chatting with their friends on Facebook. Before letting your staff loose on your expensive IT network, check that they do know their way around a computer and can at least send an email without exposing your Company to serious problems. If they don't, then give them some training before letting them go 'live' on the system.

Before they get their hands on a keyboard they should have read, understood and signed your acceptable use policies and they should understand the basics of how a virus can infect a computer, what the implications of a virus infection are and how to avoid potentially serious breaches of confidentiality when sending email to multiple recipients.

1) Sharing your distribution list

Using email to send out a newsletter, special offer or product announcement is a time saving, cost efficient method of communicating important messages to your clients. Done incorrectly however, it can reveal too much information about the people you deal with and could potentially lead to complaints about breaches of your data protection responsibilities.

Example 1

Your Company is launching a new security alarm system and you have a list of clients who have provided their email address so they can receive an update when the product is launched. They've responded to a survey that confirms that they don't currently have an alarm installed at their Company premises.

You draft an impressive sales pitch that lists the benefits of your new system and contains an effective case study showing the risks inherent in not using an alarm to instil a sense of urgency in your potential clients. You pass the email to your admin assistant who copies it into an email, pastes the whole email mailing list into the "To:" box and sends it to all of your clients.

That's fine and your email nets a load of orders. Unfortunately, one of your clients is burgled three days later and is blaming you. Why? Because every recipient of your email not only received your sales pitch, but also a full list of every Company you sent it to.

It was effectively a burglar's dream, a list of businesses who don't have an alarm installed. The client makes a complaint to the Information Commissioner's Office and your Company is fined for a serious breach of the Data Protection Act.

How could this have been avoided?

If your admin assistant had used the "Blind Carbon Copy (BCC)" field to list all of the recipients, nobody else would have been able to see the identities of the other recipients of the email.

It's a simple step but breaches of this nature happen all too frequently and it's important that your staff are trained to use the BCC facility as a matter of course when sending emails to multiple recipients.

More advanced IT users can use the mail-merge facility offered by Microsoft Word to send personalised emails to all of your clients without disclosing your mailing list. It'll also insert your client's name into the email, making it look more friendly and less like a mass mailed sales pitch.

The exact method of doing these things will vary dependant upon your email software and the version of Windows you have installed on your system. To get step by step instructions you can visit the Microsoft website and search for help for your version.

2) Incorrect use of "Reply to All"

Another potential pitfall to avoid when using email is the "reply to all" feature. Whilst this can be useful when working on collaborative projects involving lots of people who all need to be kept "in the loop" it can lead to embarrassing situations where a comment intended for only one person is inadvertently sent to everybody copied in on the original exchange.

Example 2

An important client expresses dissatisfaction with the service he's received from a member of the sales team. He sends you an email outlining his complaint and you forward it to the team member in question asking him to respond to you with his version of events. To show that you're dealing with it, you copy the client in on your request. The team member replies to the email explaining his side of the story and expressing his opinion of the client in colourful terms.

You then receive a telephone call from the irate client who tells you that he has decided to take his business elsewhere as he clearly is not valued as a customer.

What happened?

The team member inadvertently clicked "reply to all" instead of "reply" when sending his response. The customer received his comments, including the derogatory and insulting terms the salesman used to describe his client, and decided that he simply didn't want to deal with your Company any more.

How could this have been avoided?

Train your staff in the correct use of the "reply" and "reply to all" buttons when using email. They should understand the implications of inadvertently copying other parties into their communications and know that they should only use "reply all" in exceptional circumstances. As well as creating embarrassing situations such as the one outlined above, this simple mistake could result in the accidental exposure of confidential Company or client information and expose your Company to legal action.

Scam awareness training

Make your staff aware of the existence of scams and some of the forms they can take. If there are specific scams that target your industry specifically then consider bringing in a specialist to explain exactly how the scams work and the steps they can take to protect the Company from falling victim.

A blatant sales pitch from the Author

You could even buy a few copies of this book and give them to your team as required reading!

Reducing spam and scam emails

Spammers and scammers frequently use software that trawls the Internet gathering email addresses to add to their mailing lists.

To reduce the risk of this happening, you should train your employees to not publicly display their work email address on Internet forums, social media profiles or other websites.

You should also avoid listing your email address on your Company website, opting instead for a contact form that allows potential clients to send you a message without revealing your address.

If you or your staff need to publish your email address online for any reason, you should display it in the following format – yourname(at)yourdomain(dot com). That way anyone who has a genuine need to get in touch will be able to send you email but an email harvesting program won't recognise it as an email address.

These are just some of the training needs you may wish to consider. Less technically able staff may need more training than those with experience of using IT systems, however the more technically able the employee is, the higher the risk that they may become complacent and think that they don't need to consider security as much because they "know what they're doing".

Summary

Scammers are everywhere and they'll use every trick in the book to part you from your money or steal your important Company data to use to their advantage. To avoid being ripped off you'll need a combination of strong IT policies, a well configured and secure IT infrastructure and, above all, a team who are aware of the risks and able to spot a deal that seems too good to be true.

However, no matter what measures you put in place, one slip or a momentary lapse in vigilance could result in you falling victim to a scam.

The next chapter lists a number of organisations that can help you if your Company does lose money to a scammer or if you want to check out the credentials of a Company you are considering doing business with.

Where to go for help

Action Fraud

About the organisation:

Action Fraud is the national fraud reporting centre. It's the place for anyone in the UK to go for advice and information about fraud, as well as to report fraud if they've become a victim.

The Action Fraud website is full of information about different types of frauds and scams, news and alerts about some of the latest scams and an online reporting tool, which is where victims of fraud can report it.

Victims of fraud can fill out the online fraud reporting tool, or call Action Fraud if they prefer. Then they are given a crime reference number, and the case is passed over to the National Fraud Intelligence Bureau (NFIB), which is run by the police service.

After making a fraud report to Action Fraud, victims have the option of getting emotional support and practical help from the charity Victim Support

Contact Details:

Website: www.actionfraud.org.uk

Telephone: (0300) 123 2040

Police Central E-Crime Unit

About the organisation:

The Police Central E-Crime Unit (PCEU) is tasked with assisting local Police forces to investigate and prosecute incidents of computer related crime. Victims are asked to report these crimes to their local police station in the first instance. The investigating officers will contact the PCEU for advice and assistance where appropriate.

Contact Details:

The PCEU does not take reports directly from the public. Please contact your local police station.

E-Crime Wales

About the organisation:

With support from the Welsh Assembly Government, e-Crime Wales is a partnership of organisations and agencies committed to equipping Welsh businesses with the knowledge and tools to be aware, vigilant, informed and ultimately safe from the destructive effects of e-Crime in all its forms.

By bringing together the four Welsh Police Forces, specialist public sector organisations and expert commercial businesses, e-Crime Wales shares and distributes the knowledge and intelligence vital for Welsh businesses to conduct business online both safely and securely.

Website: www.ecrimewales.com

E-Crime Scotland

About the organisation:

By bringing together the Scottish Crime & Drug Enforcement Agency, the eight Scottish police forces, specialist public sector organisations and expert commercial businesses, e-Crime Scotland shares and distributes the knowledge and intelligence vital for Scottish businesses to conduct business on line both safely and securely.

Website: www.ecrimescotland.org.uk

Crimestoppers

About the organisation:

Crimestoppers is an independent charity which allows members of the public to report crime anonymously and without fear of reprisals. The information you give is passed onto the police in such a way that they do not know who you are.

Contact Details:

Website: www.crimestoppers-uk.org

Telephone: 0800 555 111

The Financial Services Authority

About the organisation:

The Financial Services Authority (FSA) regulates the financial services industry in the UK. As part of their remit they investigate financial crime including money laundering, fraud and dishonesty or market abuse. They also maintain the register of Companies authorised to carry out investment business in the UK. The register can be searched online to ensure you are dealing with a genuine organisation.

Contact Details:

Website: www.fsa.gov.uk

Telephone: 0845 606 1234 (helpline including Central Register queries)

Address: 25 The North Colonnade, Canary Wharf, London E14 5HS

Companies House

About the organisation:

Companies House maintains a database of all registered Companies in the UK and you can search the database at any time to ensure that you are dealing with a genuine business. Please note that only legally recognised Companies are listed (such as Limited Companies, PLCs or Limited Liability Partnerships). The database does not include sole traders or other unincorporated businesses such as partnerships.

Contact Details:

Website: www.companieshouse.gov.uk

Telephone: (0303) 1234 500

Scam awareness websites:

Scam Detectives

About the organisation:

Launched in January 2010, the Scam Detectives website aims to educate Internet users about the dangers of online scams, email fraud, ID theft and dodgy web-based businesses. Scam Detectives is sponsored by web design firm Clear as Crystal Web Design

Website: www.scam-detectives.co.uk

Get Safe Online

About the organisation:

Get Safe Online is a joint initiative between the UK Government, law enforcement, leading businesses and the public sector. It aims to provide computer users and small businesses with free, independent, user-friendly advice that will allow them to use the internet confidently, safely and securely.

Website: www.getsafeonline.org

Know the Net

About the organisation:

Know the net is an educational and advisory portal to help individuals or businesses. It is a public service to support and guide you through the complexities of the internet, giving advice, best practice and explanation all the way.

The aim of the website is to provide an independent, authoritative place where anyone who has concerns or questions about the internet can find reliable and impartial information on a range of topics and issues. Know the net is sponsored by Nominet.

Website: www.knowthenet.org.uk

Naked Security

About the organisation:

Naked Security is a fantastic online resource published by security software manufacturer Sophos. Voted "IT security blog of the year" by Computer Weekly readers in 2010, Sophos analyst Graham Cluley writes about the issues facing small businesses and consumers on social networking sites such as Facebook and Twitter, new virus threats and email attacks that could cost you dearly.

Website: nakedsecurity.sophos.com

Interview with a Scammer

In January 2010 scam awareness website Scam Detectives conducted an interview with reformed advance fee fraud scammer "John", who explained in some detail how the scam gangs work, how they find their victims and how other scams work.

"John" was recruited into a scamming gang at the age of 15 and was recently released from prison after serving a two year sentence for fraud, which was reduced after his co-operation with Nigerian authorities resulted in the conviction of his fellow gang members.

He described the structure of the scam gangs, and his rise from the ranks of the "foot soldiers" who earn their living gathering email addresses and sending out mass email mailshots to potential victims, earning the trust of his gangmaster or "Oga" to the point where he would be allowed to pose as a barrister or corrupt bank official to rope victims into the scam before passing them up the chain for the big score.

Scam Detectives readers were asked to submit their questions to "John" and some of these questions are listed below along with "John's" responses.

How do scammers find their victims?

First of all, the scammers need a mailing list of email addresses. They obtain this by using a specialist piece of software called an email harvester. Similar to legitimate software used by search engines, an email harvester program scours the Internet gathering email addresses posted on websites, Internet forums and guestbooks.

Once they've gathered enough addresses, the scammers will send out a mass email mailshot, often to millions of recipients, relying on only a small percentage of these producing a response.

According to "John", nine or ten of every thousand emails sent would elicit a response, with one in twenty of these responses ultimately resulting in a victim making a payment to the scammer.

How much money does the average victim lose?

Although "John" is aware of at least one victim losing over £15,000, the average scam will yield around £4,600. "John" claimed to have earned £46,000 in the year leading up to his arrest and conviction.

How do scammers convince their victims to keep sending more and more money?

By posing as bank officials, lawyers or even law enforcement officials, and using convincing fake documents including passports, share certificates, bank statements and storage manifests, the scammers are able to convince their victims that not only are they genuine, but that the problems that are preventing the release of the funds are real.

They start off asking for small amounts so as not to scare their victims off and then rely on the victim getting to the point where they have invested too much money to pull out before going for the big score.

How do scammers receive their payments?

The most popular method of receiving payments is through wire transfer services such as Western Union or Moneygram. Scammers use this method because once collected payments are virtually impossible to trace.

They may also use a network of "money mules", who believe that they are working as legitimate payment processors for International Companies. These "mules" receive cheques in the post, pay them into the bank and send the money (minus their commission) to "head office" via wire transfer. In reality, these innocent third parties are receiving payments from scam victims, and passing the money to the scammers.

What's a "Suckers List"?

As soon as you respond to a scam email (even if you don't send any money) your email address is put onto a "suckers list" of people who are likely to send cash. These lists are traded between scammer gangs for lots of money.

Lists of "suckers" who have actually sent money fetch even more cash and victims will be sent more scam emails, including recovery scams.

Are the scammers dangerous?

There have been a number of incidents of scam victims being kidnapped, robbed or even killed after being convinced to attend meetings with the scammers. You should remember that scammers are criminals and could be highly dangerous. You should be very careful when agreeing to meet a new business contact, especially overseas, especially if the deal seems dodgy or "too good to be true".

What advice can a reformed scammer give to Internet users to avoid being scammed?

- NEVER respond to a scam email, even if it's only to tell the scammer what you think of them. All you will achieve is to confirm that your email address is live and that someone reads messages sent to it and you'll receive even more scam emails. Delete the emails straight away.

- DON'T send money to anyone you don't know personally, whatever the story. Scammers will use any ruse to convince you that you will get a return on your money, but you'll never see a penny.

- If you know someone who is being scammed, they might not believe that they are a victim, even if they are shown evidence. Keep showing them articles about scams and keep trying to show them that they are being ripped off.

Final words

If you've read this far then you've learned about some of the scams and IT related threats that could be affecting your business right now. You've realised that scam victims aren't always gullible little old ladies or desperate men looking for a Russian bride to fill that hole in their life and I hope you've taken on board some of the hints and tips you can use to protect your business from those who would offer you the chance of a lifetime with one hand and mercilessly plunder your bank account with the other.

So, you can relax now safe in the knowledge that you'll never be taken in and you know every trick in the book, right? **Wrong.**

We've known about the 'flu since 1918 when veterinarian J.S.Kohen observed a disease in pigs which was believed to be the same virus as the famous "Spanish 'Flu" epidemic of the same year.

Almost 100 years later, whilst we have developed vaccinations and antibiotics to counter the illness, studies estimate that 41,000 people die from 'flu and associated complications every year in the US alone.

Why? The 'flu virus mutates and becomes resistant to the antibodies and antibiotic medicine used to combat it. Each strain becomes stronger and more resistant than the last and medical researchers are forced to play "catch-up" to find a new method of defeating the virus.

Scams and online threats evolve in a similar way. Every advance in technology brings new opportunities for the unscrupulous to take advantage of their fellow man and every book, website, newspaper article and awareness campaign warning potential victims of existing scams forces the scammer to think outside the box to come up with a new and more sophisticated method of parting you from your cash.

Your own awareness, common sense and constant vigilance is your best defence against these criminals. Whatever the story, however convincing the approach and however tempting the reward remembering one key phrase will help you to keep your hard earned cash in your pocket.

"If it seems too good to be true, it probably is"

Also available direct from the Author

The Complete IT Policy Toolkit

The average British worker spends 30 minutes a day surfing the net shopping for clothes, food and holidays during work time.

Other online activities admitted to in a survey of over 4,000 workers included:

- Instant Messaging & social networking

- Sending and receiving personal email

- Checking out porn sites

- Using online auctions

- Paying bills

- Job hunting (!)

All of these activities add up to an astonishing **90 minutes every day that YOUR staff are wasting online**. That's 43 days of productivity lost every year costing UK businesses £124 BILLION!

Not only does inappropriate use of the Internet cost your business time and money, it also puts you at risk of viruses and malware that could lead to the loss of confidential customer data or catastrophic data loss and could expose you to legal liabilities for unacceptable or illegal material downloaded onto your business machines.

The IT Policy Toolkit from Scam Detectives will help you to develop an effective IT Policy for your business which will make clear to your employees:

- What they can and cannot do when using your IT equipment to access the Internet
- What you consider to be acceptable use of Email
- How to protect your systems from Viruses & Malware
- When they can use removable media to take data away from Company premises
- What to consider when representing your business on Social Media websites
- How to use email correctly to avoid breaching client confidentiality

What's included in the toolkit?

Microsoft Word compatible policy templates covering:

» Acceptable Internet Use
» Acceptable Email Use
» Password Management Policy
» Remote Access Policy
» Remote Working Policy
» Removable Media Policy
» Mobile Phone & Handheld Device Policy

» Laptop Loan Agreement

» Social Media Guidelines

» Health & Safety for IT users checklist

Microsoft Powerpoint compatible training presentations covering:

» Protecting your systems from Viruses & Malware

» Avoiding "Phishing" Scams

» Email & Data Protection

We've also included guidance and policies for Managers on:

»Considering applications for remote working (including home working)

»Considering requests for remote access to your office network

»Monitoring employees use of the Internet & Email

»Your business data protection statement

»Health & Safety for computer users

»Agreeing the loan of laptop computers to employees

»Mobile phone & Handheld devices for drivers

The Complete IT Policy Toolkit is available to download for only £125.00 from the Scam Detectives website at:

www.scam-detectives.co.uk/blog

Scam Detectives accepts payments via secure payment processor Paypal. Your toolkit will be available for download immediately following confirmation of your payment.

If you would prefer to pay by cheque, please call our sales hotline on **0844 357 5615**

www.ingramcontent.com/pod-product-compliance
Lightning Source LLC
Chambersburg PA
CBHW081056170526
45166CB00006B/2088